All's Well

Robert Fitzgerald

All's Well
Copyright © 2019 Robert Fitzgerald

CBA Publishing Services, LLC
cbapub.com
editor@cbapub.com

First Edition 2019

ISBN-13: 978-1-7324746-9-7

Contents

Foreword

This true story of my life will appeal to some as an exciting adventure. Everyone reading this should at least find it entertaining and, in some ways, helpful. While writing this narrative, it has occurred to me that this factual story could be mistaken for a novel. Certainly, the family ancestry, the celebrity associations, and unique experiences are most often associated with fiction rather than fact. At 91 years of age, I have no need for the usual rewards of successful authorship and that should be indicated by the pamphlet reprint contained in the text. I authored the content of the pamphlets, had them printed, and then I mailed more than a thousand of them to news media and to influential people. I'm confident that everyone reviewing the pamphlet gained something from it if only to, "Keep to The Right Except When Passing."

With the dissemination of my life story, I am pleased in the belief that the story is not only entertaining but more importantly, helpful to others.

My conduct throughout ninety years has been like most people's, both good and not so good. Some people, however few, seem born to be only good. Goodness is natural for them. Maybe those of us that were not born to be naturally good, should be given even more credit for having to try harder.

Most people usually try to do the right thing and they become better as they age. A wise man once said, "All's well that ends well." Happily, my life's story is ending well.

~Robert Fitzgerald

Uncommon Ancestors

The Anton Fritz family has an interesting lineage. My mother, Anna Alosia Fritz, was born in the year 1902 in Landeck Tirol. Landeck is located in the Austrian Alps near Switzerland. Mom's father, Anton Fritz, was the illegitimate son (love child) of Franz Joseph who was Emperor of Austria and King of Hungary for 68 years. Franz Joseph married Elizabeth, Duchess of Bavaria. It was a stormy marriage. Elizabeth was quite eccentric and a frequent world traveler. Joseph, however, remained deeply attached to her until her death. She was stabbed to death by a crazed Italian in Geneva.

My grandfather, Franz Joseph's illegitimate son, was born to Theresa Fritz, daughter of the emperor's Royal Secretary. She was given a farm and a generous lifetime pension which was passed on to my grandfather. The grandmother of Franz Joseph was Maria Theresa of Austria who married the Holy Roman Emperor, Francis I.

Maria Theresa had eleven daughters and five sons. All of the daughters married Kings. One of the daughters was Marie Antoinette.

The Anton Fritz family from Austria.
Front: Lavera, Anton, Marie, Rudy, Roseina, Delores
Rear: Polly, Anna, Rose, Bertie

She was married to Louis the Sixteenth of France in 1770. The match was designed to strengthen the alliance between France and Austria. The French Revolution was brewing, and Marie Antoinette refused to accept the new restrictions imposed on her husband. Marie Antoinette proved to be stronger and more decisive than her husband, but her extravagant court expenditures and continuing intrigues helped fuel the revolution.

The monarchy was overthrown in August of 1792. Louis was executed in January of 1793 and Marie Antoinette, displaying great courage, was guillotined October 1793.

Franz Joseph's brother Maximilian became Emperor of Mexico in 1864. He had accepted the offer of the Mexican throne falsely believing that the Mexican people had voted him king. Actually, conservative Mexicans who wanted to overthrow the liberal Benito Juarez government and Napoleon who wanted to collect a debt from Mexico, made the offer.

Napoleon sent a French Army with Maximilian but withdrew the Army under pressure from the United States when the Civil War between the States ended.

Although Maximilian upheld the reform laws of the Juarez Government, he was executed by Juarez after the French Army withdrew.

My grandfather, Anton, was selected by the Hanns to marry their daughter, Roseina. Apparently, Grandfather was considered an eligible match for Roseina despite the ancestral Hanns having been awarded a Patent of Nobility by Frederick III, the last Holy Roman Emperor crowned by the Pope. It was a clandestine marriage ceremony held at four in the morning, possibly because Roseina was already pregnant. Her secret lover, a count, married to another, traveled to Chicago years later to visit Roseina and his daughter, my aunt Bertie. Bertie's son became a motion picture film director specializing in documentaries. He traveled to Austria a number of times to visit cousins and gather information. Jack's wife, Micki, had been secretary to Johnny Cash, the popular country singer. Johnny

Cash subsidized the remake by Jackie of "Stagecoach" and acted in the lead role. Mariann and I stayed with Jack and Micki in their home on the golf course in Tucson, Arizona. They both were very gracious and entertaining. Jack died of throat cancer in 2008. I have a number of letters and documents from Jack including a copy of the record listing Grandfather Anton being the illegitimate son of the emperor, Franz Joseph.

In 1906 Roseina's sister, Agnes, and her husband brought Anton, Roseina, and their seven daughters to Chicago from Austria.

In 1908 their only son, Rudolph, was born in Chicago. Roseina died of cancer in 1918. Bertha, the oldest, helped care for her siblings while they were young. They all remained close through life although Bertie and Delores eventually moved to California and Rose and LaVera moved to Minnesota. Polly, Marie, Rudy, and my mother remained in Chicago.

Rose and Polly lived to be more than 100 years old and Mom lived to be 92. Further details can be found in the chapter: "Bavaria and Austria."

The Fitzgeralds were originally Norman Knights descendants of Vikings. They went to Ireland with Strongbow following the defeat of England. At that time, they were called Geraldines. Later King Henry VI referred to Gerald Fitzgerald, the Earl of Kildare, as "The Virtual King of Ireland."

The Normans are credited by historians with bringing stability

Robert Fitzgerald

and reform to much of Europe and the near East.

Further information can be found in the chapter on Ireland.

A Great Match

After graduating from high school, my mother studied nursing at St. Elizabeth Hospital in Chicago. There she quickly became popular with both patients and staff. Mom left nursing in 1926 for homemaking when my brother Bill was born.

After Pearl Harbor in 1941, Mom returned to nursing until the war ended. Mom was short, slim and pretty. Always energetic, she was good at nursing, homemaking, cooking and raising her children.

When Mom quit nursing after the war, she often volunteered to help vaccinate school children and sometimes even obliged doctors who asked her to care for their aged parents. One cousin said that she and her siblings often called Aunt Ann for advice, particularly regarding health issues.

When in her eighties, Mom ignored her doctor's advice and had a swine flu shot which resulted in a bad reaction and she never fully recovered. Soon it became apparent that Mom was suffering from dementia and then Alzheimer's disease. The last time Mariann and I saw her, she was hospitalized and in a coma in Ft. Myers, Florida. My Brother, Bill, and his wife Colleen were living in Ft. Myers and they looked after Mom. After being on life support for a great length of time, it was agreed by all who loved her and knew her best that she would not want the tube feeding continued.

She died at the age of 92 and is still missed by many.

My father, William Fitzgerald, left the family farm at the age of twenty. He was of medium height, well-built and good looking. He always worked diligently for the family and was proud of all of us. His brothers said he was a good worker as a young man on their Indiana farm.

After high school, where he was captain of the basketball team, Dad attended Notre Dame University in South Bend, Indiana. He was there at the same time as the great Knute Rockne was coaching football for Notre Dame. Elmer Layden of the famed "Four Horsemen" was a classmate of Dad's. Eager to be independent and earn his own way, he left Notre Dame for a job at the Gary Steel Mills. Before long, his desire to succeed motivated him to leave there and start a career in sales. Buying used cars in Indiana for sale in Chicago led to meeting and eventually marrying my mother. It was a great match and the mutual love and affection between them remained strong for life.

Though Mom died when they were both 92 years of age, Dad lived another two years but dearly missed the "love of his life." While still able to care for himself, he told my brother that he wanted to die, and he died that night. As usual, Dad got what he wanted.

Bob's mother Anna

Bloom and Grow

My parents had four children; Bill born in 1926, Bob (that's me) in 1928, Mary in 1931 and Dick in 1933. Our family moved several times during the first twenty years, always to rental houses on Chicago's north side. My earliest recollections are of birthday parties, playing or fighting with brother Bill and of my father's leg breaking through the living room ceiling. Dad had mis-stepped while walking on the joists in the attic. He was athletic but apparently not nimble.

For several years the birthday cake Mom baked for me was decorated with marshmallow bunnies with paper ears and painted faces. I was fascinated with bunnies, teddy bears and my cuckoo clock. Mom made notations in the baby books she kept for each of us. One notation refers to Billy smashing my cuckoo clock with a hammer when he was five years old. Another notation mentions that I filled Billy's shoes with catsup. I don't remember which action was first but hopefully mine was in retaliation. At an early age, I showed some signs of having a flair for invention. By attaching strings to the strikers inside our piano, I was able to startle folks by causing the piano to play from my hidden position.

Bill was quite good looking, strong and athletic. His elocution ability was precocious. Still, if there was favoritism shown by our parents, it was not obvious. The first time that I felt favoritism shown was when I was about ten years old. Bill had slapped me hard on the butt with a paddle and then ran into the kitchen. I had run after him and a furious fist fight ensued. When our parents finally realized what was happening, they hurried to the kitchen from the living room. Dad helped me up from the floor. It was the third time I had been knocked down. My dad did not say a word, but Mom was very angry with me because Bill was bleeding from both his nose and mouth. Apparently, my being on the floor was not as disturbing as Bill's bleeding. I suspect that Dad was pleased since he had previously supplied boxing gloves for us to learn the "manly sport."

We always walked to school. There were no school buses that I remember in Chicago at that time. Once when entering an alleyway, an elderly man at a window about eight feet up in a building indicated that he wanted a cigarette butt lying on the ground. I obliged but he grabbed my wrist and with a surprising display of strength pulled me up. I frantically twisted my body while kicking against the building and pulled free. The experience helped make me more cautious with strangers.

A classmate died while I was in the early grades at Our Lady of Victory grammar school. Billy had been a sickly child. I was one of the pall bearers. It was a gloomy, rainy day and the dark silent cemetery was a creepy place for an eight-year-old. When we threw our gloves and a shovel full of dirt into the grave, Billy's mother wailed, "Goodbye Billy." The way it is done today with mausoleums and cremation is better.

We went to mass every morning on school days. Every class had their own set of pews and a nun assigned for that class. Tuition was $1 per month, if your family could afford it. I remember our nun reading the names of the students whose families hadn't paid. The student was to give the reason for nonpayment. A friend of mine responded, "Sister, my mom said to tell you that our ship hasn't come in yet." Even the nun laughed. I was subjected to the same embarrassment when asked why I was discontinuing piano lessons. The nuns also charged just $1 a lesson. This was during the Great Depression of the 1930's and a dollar was a significant amount for many families.

At that time, I was a first soprano in the boys' choir. We must have been good as were invited to perform on a radio program. Our classes contained up to fifty students at a time. Nevertheless, we received a good education in the basics: reading, writing, spelling, math and English grammar. Today it is surprising how many people are lacking in these skills.

All's Well

Every semester we had retreats where we were required to attend frequent church services, talks and religious films. At the conclusion, we attended mass and received special blessings. I remember the feeling of being ready to die and go directly to heaven.

Since then, my religious beliefs have been modified but I am convinced that most religions have a positive influence on society and the individual. For many, it is hard to believe with conviction in a Supreme Being, but it may be more difficult to disbelieve. Some scientists claim they do not believe in a creator, yet they believe in the symmetry of the universe. Is it then possible that all the harmony and beauty in nature, plus the instinct and intellect of animals, including humans, is merely coincidence?

Of course, there have been some big changes in the way we live since I was a boy. Then we had only fans for cooling and coal burning furnaces in the basement for heat. Mom often shoveled coal from the coal bin into the furnace. We paid extra for anthracite; a hard coal that burns cleaner. When rooms were cold, we kids sat on the radiators.

Relatives' farms, where we spent time, had no heat other than from a wood stove on the ground floor. It was necessary to sleep under thick quilts in cold weather. Oil lamps were used for lighting. The only electricity was generated by a windmill that usually produced only enough electricity for the barnyard light. Refrigerators were not yet in common use even in the city. We had an "ice box" for perishables. It had a compartment for ice with an opening to the outside porch. The iceman delivered a block of ice weekly. We did have natural gas for cooking. On the farm, dry corn cobs were used in cookstoves.

The "good old days" were not always good but it was a simpler life and it did offer some advantages. Movies were a fascination and kids loved the Saturday matinees at the local theatre with three features, news *and* sometimes on-stage contests, all for ten cents. It was also a means for parents to have a quiet, private Saturday afternoon without the kids.

We bought really good hot dogs from the little Italian man with a performing monkey chained to his cart. Women bought meat from the butcher shop and the butcher would cut the meat to order for each customer. One could get a cut with or without bone or fat in the desired size without extra charge. Butchers often supplied liver and tallow free of charge. I remember seeing wild cottontail rabbits with skins intact for 25 cents each hanging outside a store.

Some people caught fish using small explosives. Some even shocked fish by cranking a small generator such as in the old-style telephones. Not everyone would care for all of these "advantages" of the old days but there were some advantages for all, and we were conditioned to dealing with the inconveniences. Walking to school, the store and shoveling snow and coal was satisfying and the exercise was good for our health. The pace was slower, more relaxed and we did not hear much about suicides. So, even though I am glad to have today's benefits, I miss a few things from the "good old days."

When Bill was born in 1926, Mom quit nursing to become a full time stay at home mother. She was very good to us children; feeding, clothing and supervising our education as best she could. We were taken to parks, museums and zoos which were excellent at that time in Chicago. Christmases were special. We hung stockings on the fireplace mantle Christmas Eve before going to bed. We usually managed to stay in bed almost until dawn before peeking into the living room to see if Santa had come. There was always a tree there resplendent with ornaments, lights and loaded with tinsel. We rushed to open the many boxes stacked on the floor around the tree.

Our parents soon entered the scene, also "awed" by the things Santa left. We usually received the things we wanted, as well as things we needed. The stockings were filled with candy, nuts and maybe small trinkets such as whistles, pocketknives or jewelry for sister Mary. We hardly noticed that our parents were more tired than usual. Another precious holiday moment occurred when Mom took us individually to the department store where a fairy touched the chimney with a wand and a boxed gift fell out for us.

Our parents' lives centered around their children. They did not party often, we usually found enjoyment as a family. Most summers were spent at lake resorts in Wisconsin or Minnesota, except for the times when Bill and I were at an uncle's farm. We did a token amount of work on the farm like slopping the hogs or hoeing potato plants (too often hoeing out the plants).

Our uncle had a large collection of Indian arrowheads. He told us the arrowheads were sometimes exposed by plowing and by the strong winds moving the surface sand. One night, the wind was howling all night and I was eager for daylight when I could search for arrowheads. After breakfast, I ran to a particular spot I had in mind. It was a sand rise at the edge of the woods. Immediately I saw a thin piece of chipped flint protruding from the sand. With mounting excitement, I grasped it and in near disbelief pulled out a five-inch-long perfect spear head. It was the highlight of my life up to that point.

Years later I found a book listing various types of native American projectiles. The configuration of my spearhead indicates it is more than a thousand years old. I still have it displayed in a shadow box on the mantle.

For many years, we vacationed at lake resorts in Wisconsin and Minnesota. In the mornings Dad sold encyclopedia sets to the locals. In the afternoons he would swim and fish with the family. I remember Dad swimming across the lake with me either on his back or chest alternatively when I was little. When he finished with an area, we would move to another lake area.

Bill and I always had a motorboat to use and we spent many hours fishing, spearing fish, swimming and exploring. We often engaged in the "King of the Hill" contests where the object was to push or knock your opponent with an oar into the water. When our opponent was out of the boat, we tried to start the motor and speed away before he could get back into the boat. It was often dangerous, but we were never seriously hurt.

Sometimes people would be frightened by bears when going to the outhouse at night. Once, a local farmer came into the lodge to say that a bear was eating one of his hogs. There was a $15 bounty on bears at that time in Minnesota. Several of us went out in the dark with guns looking for the bear; fortunately for the bear, we did not find it. A few nights later, Bill and I were heading back to the cabin from a small isolated lake when we saw a bear swimming behind us. Only the top of his head was visible in the light of the moon. We circled the bear repeatedly while I hit it with a heavy "hand hewn" oar. Finally, the bear went under near the shore. The resort owner, a Swedish Native American mix, retrieved the bear using a large grappling hook. It was a large bear, but the $15 bounty paid for tanning the hide for mounting.

Another time as a teenager, I spent several hours on the roof of the cabin to discourage a bear that came in the night and clawed holes in the porch screening. I had a gun but did not need it. For my twelfth birthday, Mom had given me a shotgun. Yes, our parents were somewhat permissive and overconfident, but I was always careful with guns. I initially hunted pheasants, rabbits, squirrels and ducks. Later I also hunted deer and wild turkeys. About the age of thirty, I started practicing with a bow and arrow and became a quite accurate archer and taking down both deer and turkey.

I gave up hunting deer in my eighties. I am ninety years old now and still able to hunt once in a while. Two years ago, while standing up entering a duck blind in the backwaters of a river, I capsized my one-man duck boat in 4½ feet of water. I went underwater to retrieve my gun and other gear. My arthritic knees caused the boat to wobble when I stood up. Fortunately, it was not freezing weather.

Athletes and Outdoor Adventures

When I was about ten years old, Bill and I joined a fight club of sorts. We boxed frequently with a group of friends. I was two or three years younger than the others, so I imagine most of them held back when boxing with me. I am sure Marty Wendell held back. He was the best athlete of the group and a great guy. Marty was a future All American football player at Notre Dame and then a linebacker for years for two different NFL teams. As kids, we had a prairie league football team. One day Marty and I were walking through a prairie when we met an older boy we knew as "Whitey." He said, "Marty your team could not be very good if this little kid plays on it." Marty replied, "I bet you can't run through him." I stopped Whitey in his tracks both times he tried. Maybe it surprised even Marty a little because he would bring it up every time we met afterwards.

The last time I saw Marty was around 2010. He drove out to Apple Canyon Lake to see Bill and me. He and Bill were teammates on the St. George High school team that won the National Championship in 1943. Marty brought two of my former teammates with him from Chicago. We had played a final game together for the Chicago Championship at Soldier's Field. I played with my left arm chained at the wrist to my waist. I had been having shoulder dislocations when the arm was raised above my chest.

We met for lunch at the lakeside restaurant and afterwards went to our nearby homes to see the women. As they were leaving to return home, Marty said, "Bob, you taught me how to tackle." What a great compliment from a pro! Instinctively, I would meet the runner moving as fast as I could and hit him hard and low with my shoulder while pulling his legs up and grasping him from below the knees. When unable to run, simply pulling up the legs is still best. Marty did not look well. He was pale and I wondered if all the head banging as a linebacker was the cause. Marty died about a year later.

When the polio epidemic hit Chicago in the 1940s, we moved to Bangs Lake, Wauconda, Illinois to escape the threat. I was about ten years old when we moved again to Webster Groves, a suburb of St. Louis, Missouri. Mariann Stilwell, who I would marry eighteen years later, would attend Webster College in the future. Webster College is close to where I lived in Webster Groves and it was to be one of the few times Mariann would cross my trail before we met.

Brother Bill was still my only companion. I was a loner, shy and maybe somewhat odd. Eventually I overcame my shyness, but I am not sure about the odd. An entry in my baby book states, "Bobby can hold his own very well, does not stand for any abuse from his brother but uses his right effectively." There are other later indications that I have a warrior personality. At about the age of twenty, I jumped off the rear platform of a trolley car in Chicago about two in the morning to confront a man that appeared to be attacking a woman. When I grabbed him, the woman began hitting me with her purse. I guess they had been out drinking too.

Another time, while at the University of Illinois in Champaign, Illinois, an army air corpsman picked a fight with me outside of a roadhouse. Because of my bad shoulder I could only use the left to block punches. He gave me a bloody nose and I tackled him, held him down and let blood drip on his uniform. His companion told my buddy that it was the first time his friend had lost a fight. He was the corps champ in his division, which I would guess was light heavyweight. Fighting with just one good arm is not smart and I have been lucky to get away with it. Personality, however, is difficult to change.

I had an initial experience with gals in Webster Groves. They wanted to play doctor with Bill and me but settled for kissing games. They only wanted to kiss Bill, but he told them they would have to kiss me too. I submitted and I had no further interest in kissing for many years.

We stayed in Webster Groves only through the summer and then returned to Chicago when the polio problem had lessened. We then moved from Our Lady of Victory parish to another northwest side location. There I attended sixth grade at St. Ferdinand's, a BVM nuns' school. They were strict and good teachers. The first day there, at recess, some of the boys tried to instigate a fight between me and their champion. He was big but fortunately for one of us, did not want to fight. My homeroom nun heard about it and pulled me out of the classroom demanding to hear the details. She was more intimidating than the "champion" had been.

There were some occurrences that summer that stayed in my memory. My sister, Mary, who was then nine years old, wanted to play cops and robbers. Mary seemed to like being frightened when playing the game. One day in the basement playing cops and robbers, I took her prisoner, locked her in the "execution shed" and blew fumes from sulfur burning in a tube into the "chamber." Apparently, it was more frightening than desired. Mary screamed loud enough for Mom to hear from upstairs. She came charging down the stairs as I was releasing the prisoner; I got a hard slap in the face for adding such a realistic touch to our game. It was the only time I was ever hit by my parents.

Shortly thereafter, I helped save Mary when she burst into the kitchen wide-eyed, pointing to her throat. Mom shouted for me to hold Mary upside down and then slapped Mary's back. A jawbreaker gumball popped out; it had been lodged in Mary's windpipe.

That summer, Bill and I had our last physical confrontation. He found that I could now hold my own and we stuck to a truce from then on. That fall I transferred to Mary Lyon Public school. My math class was taught by a beefy woman with bulging eyes. Early on she called on me to answer a question. I hadn't been paying attention; a frequent occurrence for me. I was told to come to the front of the room and apologize. When I stood mute, the teacher grabbed me by the ear and marched me to the principal's office where I was told to have my mother come for a conference the following day. Mom came and was told that I was not yet ready for that class. Fortunately, the annual aptitude test given a few days later proved them wrong. Another boy and I got the highest grades on the test. From then on, I paid more attention and was called on frequently.

Another teacher for art and culture was more to my liking. She was elderly and seemed eccentric but very talented. She orchestrated the graduation ceremony with an extravaganza that included our class singing the Alleluia Chorus in four parts. I was considered a soprano although by then I was more of a tenor. She was also poetic and had the class memorize several "Memory Gems." I still remember some of them word for word: "The heights of great men reached and kept are not attained by sudden flight but while their neighbors slept were toiling upward in the night," and, "Their noon day never knows what names immortal are, Tis night alone that shows, how star surpasses star."

After I graduated from Mary Lyon, we moved to the far northside and Dad enrolled Bill and I at St. George High in Evanston,

Illinois. The school was about a mile walk from the end of the Chicago streetcar (trolley line). Dad had first convinced the principal of a public school not in our district to allow us to enroll there. He told him that we were good kids, and most importantly, good football players, the latter talent not yet proven. Of course, the school had a winning football team. I don't know why Dad changed his mind and enrolled us instead at St. George, but it proved to be the right choice, especially for football fame.

As a transferee from another high school, Bill was ineligible to play football his junior year. He had played at Steinmetz and tied the school record for the 100-yard dash. Bill did play, together with Marty Wendell, in his senior year. At that time, the enrollment at St. George was only 410 students. St. George was a boy only Christian Brothers' school. It did not have a reputation as a good football school, but the Brothers sought to change that. With a new coaching staff, St. George won all but one game during the season.

The playoff game for the Chicago Catholic League title ended in a tie. A flip of a coin decided that St. George would compete against the public league champ for the Chicago Area title. The Public League champ, Wendell Philips High School, was an all-black school on Chicago's south side. It had a total enrollment of over 4000 boys and girls. There were no divisions in those days. The big schools also played the small schools. Today, there are up to eight size divisions and schools only compete with schools in their division.

All's Well

Buddy Young, the star player for Wendell Philips, held the world record for the 100-yard dash. Their team had not even been scored on during the season. Their Victory March plans were printed in the Chicago Tribune prior to the game. The championship game for the Chicago area, called the Kelly Bowl, because Kelly was the mayor of Chicago that year, was played at Soldiers' Field. There was a record standing room only crowd of over 100,000 in attendance for the game. Bill and Marty played linebackers and were able to contain Buddy Young's end runs. St. George won, 19-12, in spite of Buddy Young and the fact that Phillip's line averaged thirty pounds per man heavier than St. George's starting line. Buddy Young went on to play successfully for the NFL until he died in a car crash a few years later. St. George went on to beat St. Michael in NYC (champs for 5 straight years). St. George was then heralded as the National High School Football Champion.

For the first three years at St. George, I was consistently on the National Honor Society List. The Brothers were good teachers; they were tough, and the students respected them. Our new coach, Max Burnell, a former Texan, was young and athletic. He had been a substitute running back for the Chicago Bears. At St. George he was in charge of football, track and physical education classes. During a P.E. class I jumped over twenty feet and Max asked me to join the track team. That year I tied the school record for the fifty-yard dash at 5.4 seconds and won first place in the broad jump at the city track championship meet. Today the "broad jump" is called the long jump.

Keeping fit for track and football was not fun and I had other interests including hunting and fishing. By missing the next summer football camp, I showed a less than compelling desire to play. I had been doing well as a running back, but missing camp caused me to lose my position as starting halfback. Larry Coutre, who later made All American at Notre Dame and Don Dufeck, future All American at Michigan were now the leading backs and there were other good backs on the team as well.

I was allowed back on the team that fall and tested at the guard position. In those days we played both offense and defense. I looked smaller but weighed about 185 pounds and was strong and quick. Some of the senior linemen were big and veterans from the 1943 championship team, but I did well against them. We lost our first game and the coach was so angry he called a special meeting for the next day. I arrived on the field late as the coach was haranguing the team. I joined the group and when Burnell finally noticed me he shouted, "Fitzgerald, you're late! Turn in your equipment." I stayed, assuming he was not serious—just very angry. On further consideration, I decided that hunting, with the hunting season starting, overruled being in the coach's doghouse and I walked off and turned in my equipment. When Burnell realized what I did, he announced that I would never again be on one of his teams.

After football season, however, I learned that Burnell had

arranged for a summer job for the team with the Milwaukee R.R. When I asked to be included, he said I could, if I competed in the city track finals to be held soon. I competed in the broad jump but without practice, my timing was off and I missed the take-off board on my first attempts. The rain was an added problem. On my final attempt, I leapt in front of the board to have a qualifying jump—I took third place, a disappointment since I had won the event the previous year. Coach Burnell was good at arranging summer employment for our team. One summer we sold programs at Dyke Stadium in Evanston for Northwestern College football games for 25 cents. Northwestern College had almost eight female students for every male student and their football teams were not very good. Then, Ara Parseghian was hired to coach and recruit players. He was so successful that Notre Dame finally hired him to prevent further losses to Northwestern.

The railroad job was a farce. We all went swimming in a nearby farm pond much of the time. We were supposed to be checking the brackets securing the rails to the oak ties, but none of them needed fixing. Finally, we were all fired but only because a team member, a notorious trickster, trapped some railroad officials in the smoke-filled station. He had used the woodstove to fill the station with smoke and then held the door closed so the men could not escape. The knave that caused us to lose our jobs was a valuable player for the team and there was no punishment that I know of. Ironically, he later became a Christian Brother. He came to our wedding ten years later. Mariann's aunt recognized him and chided him about the times he had disrupted things at her hamburger stand years before. He claimed to still be doing penance for it. "All's well that ends well."

Brother Bill was sometimes rebellious as a teenager. The Brothers quickly slapped him down, but it took a punch in the nose to change him at home. I think it was the only time that Dad ever hit Bill and Bill reacted by trading blows with Dad. My siblings and I restrained Bill until he came to his senses. Dad summoned Bill to a talk the next day. It was routine for Bill, but I never had one. I believe however, that I was also both good and bad, dumb and smart, like I think most people are.

As a teenager, I became more socially motivated, but I still did not look for new friends, especially girls. Maybe I was still too shy. However, at least two different girls took the initiative when I was home alone. One of the visits I remember resulted only in kissing; the other went further.

We know that the brains of adolescents are not fully developed. It seems also that the brains of some males take longer to develop than female brains. I suspect that many football players are also in this category. This suspicion may be because football players were my usual companions during the early years. Sometimes we were naughty, maybe even coming close to committing a misdemeanor. The fact that we were being taught and disciplined by Christian Brothers and reciting a classroom prayer to begin the day did not always define or refine us.

One summer before my senior year, several teammates and I were staying for the weekend at the lake region in northern Illinois. During the night, two of us went to buy beer. We "borrowed" a rowboat that was docked on a long channel leading to the tavern. Unable to convince the bartender that we were of age, we left without the beer. As we were rowing back toward the dock, I saw a car stopped on the bridge ahead. It was a very dark night, but I was almost sure it was the police searching for us. We abandoned the boat and fled across country. As we neared our cabin, a car with very bright lights was slowly coming toward us. We laid face down in the ditch while the car passed by. Fortunately for us, the deserted road had no streetlights. Were we lucky that night; or was there some divine intervention because we were good Christian boys, most of the time?

That fall I was duck hunting on the Mississippi between Savanna, Illinois and the Quad cities. My partner and I were in a camouflaged boat at the Iowa shoreline on the edge of a refuge. A flock of ducks coming from Illinois passed high overhead. My partner said, "They're too high," but I shot anyway and dropped one. It fell into the few mallard decoys we had placed close to shore. I propped its head up with a forked stick pushed into the mud. The current close to shore was very slow but eventually it carried the duck slowly away. It was during the week and there were no other hunters in sight, so I let the duck drift a bit. Then a motorboat with two hunters appeared in the distance. They were headed our way, so we untied our boat and headed out to get the duck. The hunters got to the duck first and the big guy picked it up. I stopped our motor and said, "It is our duck, a black duck." He replied, "No, it is a hen mallard." I told him he was wrong, and he knew it belonged to us.

By that time, we were alongside the other boat and the unsportsmanlike guy said, "Possession is nine tenths of the law." I grabbed the duck out of his hands and he then tried to grab it back. I shoved him hard with my hands to his chest and he spun around and almost went into the water. As he recovered, he grabbed his shotgun. My partner said aloud, "I wouldn't do that." It may have saved us from a catastrophe. I was also concerned about the teenager in the boat that also had a shotgun, but he did not move. The would-be tough guy, looking very angry and embarrassed in front of the kid said, "Let's settle this on shore." Silly pride made me respond, "Ok, follow me." Fortunately, he went in the opposite direction. When we unloaded at the dock in the evening, the tough guy was there with some buddies. Nothing was said.

Sometimes, my brain worked well. I was driving my dad's DeSoto in the early morning from Chicago to the Mississippi for another hunt. It was dark and raining and I was alone. Suddenly the engine quit, and the gas pedal went soft. I suspected the linkage had disconnected and I coasted onto the shoulder and engaged the emergency brake. With a flashlight I walked back along the road looking for anything that might be part of the linkage. After one hundred feet or so, I saw a large cotter pin that had never been spread open. When I got under the car, I found that it was for connecting the arms of the linkage. After inserting the cotter pin through the linkage connections, I spread it open with my knife. That time my brain was working well, but I also needed a lot of luck.

It was my good fortune when Jack, a big Irishman and student at St. George took an interest in me. Jack kept me busy in the constant pursuit of interesting things to do. Together we served as instructors at a YMCA summer camp in Michigan, made several canoe trips into the Quantico Superior National Parks (Boundary Waters), many basketball evenings at the Y, a few mixers with girls' schools, outdoor shows, road trips, pool and some elbow bending at favorite hangouts when we were high school seniors.

Jack forced me into social awareness and got me involved in interesting activities. He was the instigator and I never needed another friend. When Jack died at the age of twenty-two, I reverted to being a loner.

To this day, I usually hunt or fish and spend my free time alone. I've never gotten in the habit of phoning others to get together. I guess I am still a loner as I am content to do things without company. I don't know if that is an asset or not but at least there's no chance of disagreements with others when there are no others involved.

Jack and I first met Bill, the canoe trip outfitter from Ely,

Minnesota, at an outdoor show in Chicago. He showed us film of the numerous lakes and rivers in the two adjacent national parks belonging to the U.S. and Canada. The combined parks contain a vast wilderness area that takes days to cross by canoe. Both parks are open to those that register at entry points. Flying in is not permitted now, but it was then. Over the years with others I made several canoe trips there. Usually we made ten or more portages to reach base camp. Once there, the tent was erected, and a fire hole dug for the kettle. We often fished and explored until evening and we cooked the evening meal before leaving camp in the morning. It could be noodles, cheese and spam boiled and placed in the fire hole after covering the coals with sand, gravel and dirt. The covered pot was then packed with moss and leaves. It was nice to have a hot meal ready to eat when we returned tired and hungry.

We could always catch more fish than we needed. Northern pike and Walleyes were abundant and in early season, we caught lake trout by trolling.

We often had shore dinners around midday. Fish just caught were roasted over the fire on spits. Sometimes I filleted the fish and coated them with flour, then fried them in bacon grease in a small pan we carried along. Other times we simply had hardtack, cheese and raisins for lunch. The lakes were crystal clear, and we drank the water with a tin cup without bothering to purify it. None of us ever got sick on the trips.

Bob during first canoe trip in the
Boundary waters around 1946

Bob Henn and Bob Fitzgerald
Minnesota and Canada Border

Bob holding a walleye on one
of his first canoe trips

One year when it was still legal to fly into the parks, the outfitter suggested we use an axe on a competitor's rowboats that we were going to pass by. We found the boats, there were eight or more, but we did not harm them. We never had a problem with wildlife, although there were wolves and black bear around. Bill had photos in his shop of wildlife and trophy fish from the park. In one photo, he was standing next to his plane with five dead timber wolves. There was a $50 bounty on wolves at the time.

One of my last canoe trips after I was discharged from the army was with my brother Dick. While taking turns paddling and casting along the shoreline for Northern pike, we caught three over thirty-eight inches long in one afternoon. When we arrived back at the camp, it was getting too dark for photos, so we left the fish in the water on a stringer. In the morning a very large snapping turtle had claimed the fish and hissed at me as I approached. I shot the turtle intending to butcher it for cooking, but our axe and knives were too dull for removing the shell. We had forgotten to bring sharpening file and stone, so we buried the remains.

During the course of many trips, I developed my own technique for controlling the canoe as the stern paddler. I drew the paddle under the canoe and brought it out of the water behind the canoe with the blade up. This way there is no appreciable turning of the bow as in the J stroke and no slowing of the momentum. Years later I was told by the manager of a canoe dealership on the Fox Lake chain in Illinois that my idea was now the popular method used by experienced canoeists.

My best friend Jack was not around for the last few canoe trips. He had been studying architecture at the University of Illinois in Champaign. Jack had already won the Beaux Arts Award for Design and was beginning his last semester when a phone call from Champaign came for my sister Mary. She had been dating Jack and may have been waiting for his call. Mary was talking with our parents when the phone rang. Before answering Mary exclaimed, "Jack's dead!" ESP? Unfortunately, she was right. It was a friend of Jack's calling to report that Jack died in an automobile accident.

At one time, I was somewhat skeptical about ESP. Now, the experiences of several close associates convinced me that it is real. The subject is fascinating and a great mystery. That's why clairvoyants are called mystics. The subject supports belief in the spirit world and in a Supreme Being.

My wife, Mariann, consulted an astrologer at a Psychic Fair when our children were teenagers. She was told she was an only child, her parents separated when she was an infant. The psychic also said, correctly, that we had taken in a foreigner and stated the correct year it happened. Then she told Mariann that we were having problems with our eldest son and that he and I were "butting heads." At that, Mariann said there was a very long pause. Finally, the psychic said it would get much worse before it got better. Our oldest son was killed a short time thereafter. Everything the psychic told Mariann was correct.

My brother Bill, myself and others I know had similar experiences with readers, mystics, astrologists and clairvoyants that have revealed the "unknown." Some friends of ours believe the Ouija Board can help communicate with the spirit world. I am still somewhat skeptical about that one, but a respected priest advised against using the Ouija board.

One summer our parents took Mary and Dick with them to Minnesota. Bill and I had summer jobs at home. My job was helping the grounds keeper at a large cemetery on the north side of Chicago. Small ponds in the cemetery were occasionally used by Mallard ducks and there were a lot of pheasants that roosted in the lower tree branches. The cemetery was close to home and eventually I made a few forays into it at night to hunt. There was a ten-foot-high concrete wall along the cemetery's closest side. It was an isolated area without streetlights. The wall had a projecting ridge near the base that I used as a springboard to leap up and get a hold on the top of the wall and then pull myself up and over. The few excursions netted one Mallard and several pheasants; all dressed, roasted and eaten by Bill and me that summer.

My little brother Dick would be six feet tall, 190 pounds and a record-breaking fullback for the St. George football team as a senior. At the age of twelve, however, Dick was plump, plodding and too timid. I noticed that he did not stand up for himself when challenged by his peers, so I convinced him to follow a training program. First, I had Dick run through the alley with me. He was slow enough then that I could run alongside backwards while urging him on. Boxing with gloves on was another important part of the program. As he improved, I would occasionally hit a little harder. If he whimpered, I would give him a pep talk and then we would continue with the lesson. Finally, I arranged a boxing match between Dick and his chief abuser. Bill was the abuser's second and I was Dick's. We set up a makeshift ring and talked the abuser into taking part in the contest. Dick did well but the abuser may have held back somewhat. As promised, Dick got all the banana splits he wanted and regardless of who was best, his confidence improved. He was now in better condition and emerging from the baby phase. Dick played basketball his next two years in grammar school and did well.

The first sign of a problem with my shoulder came when I was about seventeen years old. When boxing with a friend, I got sharp pains in the shoulder when striking with my left. The first dislocation occurred when boxing in a school tournament; then again when swimming across a channel. Dave, the center on our football team forced it back into place. Thereafter, Dave forced it back when necessary during football practice and the team doctor followed Dave's method when it happened during the game on Sundays. They caused the condition to worsen. After a special harness failed, our coach had my wrist chained to a belt around my waist while playing. If necessary, to fight in self-defense, I could still punch with a strong right arm and block punches with my left. Of course, I tried to avoid anything that might cause another dislocation. I often slept with my left wrist tied to the bottom of the bed so I wouldn't raise my arm too high while sleeping. I have been careful and had only two dislocations since high school.

The first was in 1946. Three of us were walking along a busy street in Chicago at night. It was after the war had ended the year before and a lot of veterans were still out hitting the bars. As we passed, I heard two guys threatening an old couple. One said that the two of them could lick all the Jews in the neighborhood. I stopped to be sure of what was happening. One of the guys reached out to include me and repeated, "The three of us can lick all you Jews." I said, "No, I am with them." He then tried to push me away and I punched him in the jaw. He was knocked back against the tavern's plate glass front. As he bounced off the glass, I hooked him with my left, momentarily forgetting the injury to that shoulder. My shoulder joint dislocated and I was virtually helpless, but my buddies came back to rescue me. When we left the scene, a crowd had gathered and was threatening the Jew baiters. Maybe friend Jack had tipped them off.

In my senior year at St. George, our football team was the favorite to win the Catholic League Championship. We fell behind late in the game and lost. There were two obvious reasons for our less than usual winning performance. Coutre, our best running back, broke a bone in his foot and most of us had contracted the flu bug several days prior to the game. A few days after the game, a teammate brought a bottle of booze to school and four of us had a swig from it. We were caught by a Brother and given a warning that we would be expelled if there was another serious violation.

Soon after that, there was a basketball pep rally held in the gym. Everyone was to attend. I was with a friend who prevailed on me to wait while he had a quick smoke in a seldom used part of the school building. A Brother saw us leaving the woman's washroom followed by a cloud of cigarette smoke. The school Director sent for us and we were told to pack our things. My partner said, "Fitz was not smoking." It did no good.

I needed a credit and a half for admission to the new Chicago branch of the University of Illinois. Brother Bill advised that I could take accelerated courses at the YMCA downtown for the credits. When I finished the courses which included typing, all my credits were accepted by the U of I and I was even exempted from some of the usual prerequisites. Apparently, I was not mature enough yet for college. After dislocating my shoulder in a physical ed class, I quit going to classes for a time and was expelled. I hadn't notified the proper authorities that I had been incapacitated by the injury. I would have to wait for two semester for readmission.

I applied for a teller's position at a north side bank in Chicago and was required to take a lie detector test. Previously, I had read about a man beating the polygraph by concentrating on erotic thought only and answering questions immediately. It helps to anticipate what will be asked and have a ready response. I was not sure that I would keep the job long. For one thing, my best friend Jack had proposed that we apply for a summer job as instructors at a YMCA camp in Michigan. Of course, I also intended to return to college when able. I passed the test and was given the job of assistant to the currency teller. We worked in a barred cage with drawers containing all the denomination of coin and currency including $1000 bills. As summer approached, I decided to apply with Jack for the YMCA.

The camp was on a small private lake and I was given the job of fishing instructor. Early on, a ten-year-old boy was damaged by a fly rod that I was using to teach the art of fly casting. I asked to be transferred to nature studies. That did not work out well either. While leading a group of boys through the woods on a trail, I heard yelling at the rear of the line. As successive boys began yelling, I realized what happened and shouted for everyone to run after me. Everyone but me was stung, I think. Later, I learned the rear boy had been beating the wasp nest with his staff.

While I led the troop back to the camp walking in the shallow water near shore, another boy screamed. He had stepped on a muskrat trap that pinched his foot through his tennis shoe. At the end of the season, I did not get the award for best and most popular counselor but both Jack and I did get Red Cross Lifeguard Instructor certification.

All's Well

Months later, Jack and I hitched to a small northwest Illinois town to visit the two brothers we met at the Y camp. The brothers wanted to attend a local dance that night. It was held in the community building and there was a piano on the stage. We had been drinking whiskey. Jack asked me to play Danny Boy. While playing, the sheriff announced it was closing time. He dragged me off the piano bench before I finished the piece. Impulsively, I got him in a headlock and when I eased off he started choking me with his huge hand. Jack interceded and the sheriff released his grip on my throat. He told us to report to his office in the morning. Instead, we left town early. Maybe that was what the sheriff expected us to do.

My next job was driving a taxicab in Chicago. I enjoyed it and stayed with it for more than a year. The money was good for a single guy living with his parents and I learned a lot about the city and met some interesting people.

In 1950, I was drafted into the army for the Korean conflict and sent to Ft. Leonard Wood, MO for basic training. One night the sergeant announced there would be an eight-mile march leaving at 4 AM the next morning. When the company left on schedule, two of us weren't ready. No one checked and when packed we went out to the main road and flagged down an army truck. After a few miles, we passed our company and, lying low in the back of the truck, continued on over the next hill. Then, we knocked on the cab's rear window, stopped, thanked the driver and ran into the woods along the road.

After the column passed, we joined the stragglers. Our success helped lessen the feeling of having lost our independence.

There was a need for cadre at the time and we were all tested for placement. I was offered "Officers Training" but it required signing on for additional time in the service, so I turned it down and opted for the Army Security Agency. In the ASA, trainees were sent to Ft. Devens at Ayer, Massachusetts. There we spent several hours a day typing the messages transmitted in Morse Code. To graduate it was required to correctly type out messages sent at the rate of twenty-five words a minute. That's about double the speed most operators are capable of receiving. At Devens I was allowed frequent weekend passes. I went fishing and even crow hunting with a young man living in Ayer with his parents and sister. They were a handsome and friendly family and I joined them for Sunday dinner in their home. I assume the special treatment was because I was in the service at that time of war. Mom had shipped my fly rod and shotgun to me. I don't remember where I kept them. It is possible that my commanding officer allowed me to keep them, broken down, in my locker.

The first time I was thanked for my service was after the Vietnam War. It took me by surprise, and I blurted out, "It was a pleasure." After that I was prepared and would simply reply, "Thank you." The military draft was discontinued after "Nam" and now thanking a vet for their service is perhaps even more appropriate because all military personnel are volunteers.

All's Well

Just as I was about to reach the goal of 25 words a minute, I had a seizure. It was a shock. I had never had one before and now I was unable to use my hands properly. They took me to the field hospital where I was examined and assigned to a bed. The following day I was given a thorough exam at the Naval hospital in Chelsea, Mass. Back at the field hospital in Ft. Devens, while awaiting the test results, I was offered some interesting therapy choices; these included attending a Boston Pops concert, the Red Socks baseball games, and a boat trip along the Cape Cod Coast. I took the boat trip. There were many picturesque little fishing villages along the sandy coastline, and it was an enjoyable day. After a week or more there was still no word on the test results, so I asked to be returned to duty. I had already missed graduating with the first class. I soon graduated and was sent to Ft. Bragg, N.C. for maneuvers. We first stopped at a security facility in Virginia. One of our group was bounced out of the ASA there. I suspect he said the wrong thing to a couple we met there in a bar.

During maneuvers we camped in the woods and I got a bad case of ivy poisoning. I was on the night shift receiving transmissions in a small darkened trailer. The heat and humidity made the itch worse and it lasted for several days. When maneuvers ended, we were told to pack for transport to the Far Eastern Command, meaning Korea. First, I checked with the field hospital and was told that the colonel in charge wanted to see me. It was just a short way and I walked there. The colonel was direct; he asked me if I wanted a discharge. Of course, my wishes wouldn't have mattered. The report from the Naval Hospital in Chelsea had just arrived and x-rays confirmed that I had a significant head injury. The Draft Board in Chicago had been notified about the injury before induction, but it was not even a consideration apparently. Concentration on the constant high-speed transmissions aggravated the condition and caused the seizure. The head injury had originally been caused by a crushing blow during a fracas at an upscale bar. Two friends and I had stopped there to meet someone following a wedding celebration. Ever since, my cognitive response is slow and sometimes I experience tremors on the left side of my face. Before receiving the medical discharge, I was hospitalized for several days. After signing a form releasing the Army from liability, I was given funds for travel to Chicago. I arrived home just before Christmas.

Sy and Meg DeVry, good friends of my parents and next-door neighbors, took us all out to celebrate. Sy and his brother Bill owned the DeVry-DeForest School known for technical training. DeForest had invented the vacuum tube that made television possible.

Sy and Meg were Illinois University grads and avid Illinois football fans. Late,r when 50 different colleges were trying to recruit Dick for their football teams, DeVry's had a big party for Dick. Jack Dempsey was their PR man and Dick had photos taken with Dempsey and my dad.

At the time, I was attending classes at the University of Illinois and two of the football coaches sought my help in recruiting Dick.

They told me that my brother Bill had been one of the best fullbacks Illinois ever had before his knee was permanently injured.

Dick ultimately signed with Notre Dame which several of his friends were attending. During his senior year at St. George High, Dick scored 31 touchdowns for the Illinois state record. Great offers were made. The University of Michigan brought the family to their campus in a private railroad car for their recruiting efforts. During the hoopla, Notre Dame made no effort to contact Dick. Finally, Moose Krause, ND's Athletic Director, phoned to invite my dad and Dick to South Bend for dinner with he and Frani Leahy. Dad countered, inviting them to our house for dinner.

Leahy, winner of four national football championships, came with Krause and entertained the family at length with stories. Dick accepted the offer of a six-year scholarship to study Business Administration. Dick did well both in football and academically, graduating in the top 10% of his class. He received invitations to play in both Blue-Gray and East-West Bowl Games. He chose only the Blue-Gray contest.

Athletic scholarships at Notre Dame are relatively modest and recipients are required to maintain a good scholastic record. With only about 13,000 students, both sexes combined, Notre Dame still managed to field competitive teams against much larger schools.

After graduating, Dick was drafted into the military to play for Navy. Marty Wendell had gone the same route years earlier, playing for Navy and being instrumental in a rare defeat of Notre Dame, his alma mater.

After Dick was discharged, he was offered a contract by George Halas to play for the Chicago Bears. The Bears already had Alex Casares, one of the best fullbacks in the league. After only five games, Halas wanted to make a trade with the Steelers which would include Dick. He had enough football by then, so Dick quit and went to Sun Valley Idaho where he became the company accountant for the resort. Dick was then recruited to manage a popular restaurant lounge in Ketchum, Idaho. There Dick met Ernest Hemingway and became an occasional fishing partner with the big man.

Former St. George High School Stars (left to right)
Marty Wendell, All American, Notre Dame, NFL Linebacker
Bill Fitzgerald, Linebacker, 1943 United States High School Champions
Dick Fitzgerald, Illinois High School Scoring Champion, All American,
Notre Dame, Chicago Bears
Bob Fitzgerald, "One Arm" Guard, quit football after championship
game in Soldier's Field, Chicago

All's Well

Next, Dick traveled to Spain where he ran with the bulls at Pamplona and then broke a leg skiing. From Spain, Dick went to Colorado where he met and married Sally Yonkers, another ski bum. Dick was now more than thirty years old. Sally and Dick raised two boys and a girl. Their son, Steven, was All-State in hockey and football. Steven's son was All-State in football and Lacrosse.

Aspen was growing fast. Soon after Dick and Sally married, Dick got into the real estate business. He worked hard, studied real estate law and hired a couple of former NFL football stars to work with him. Fitzgerald Realty became the leading realtor in Aspen and Dick did very well financially and retired at an early age.

Now that I was qualified for the G.I. Bill, I was eager to enroll at the University of Illinois main campus at Urbana-Champaign. It was not as easy as I hoped. After checking my record at their Chicago branch, the board rejected my application. Brother Bill came to my aid. An influential dean and drinking buddy of Bill's cleared the way, provided I scored well on the aptitude test given by the Illinois Institute of Technology in Chicago. After taking the test, I was admitted but required to maintain a "B" average grade until graduating.

For the next three years I lived on campus during the regular school year. The first year, I roomed upstairs in a family home next door to a Jewish sorority. Several other young men also had rooms there. The girls next door could be spied on through an attic window, but one of the guys tipped them off. Still, some of the girls did not care, were unaware or maybe exhibitionists. I tried it once but quit soon. It was uncomfortable laying pone in the cramped quarters.

During this time, I had two meal jobs at different sororities, including the one next door. There were usually four of us guys to serve food, bus tables and do the dishes. We were well fed at both sororities and the girls were friendly, but I don't remember anything between us. Vets that were attending schools on the G.I. Bill at the time received $110.00 a month from Uncle Sam. The next two years, two friends and I rented a house and I cooked the evening meals. They were supposed to clean up and do the dishes, but Al and Charlie clearly weren't always prompt or effective doing their jobs. Eventually I made the trip to Mexico with Charlie. Al was good looking, an excellent boxer and always seemed happy. He failed to graduate and several years later committed suicide by jumping from a fifth story window. I have no idea why Al wanted to die. He was a great guy and very popular.

I dated a few times, but the girls seemed immature. I did not have a strong incentive to keep at it, but one day I was surprised to meet a former girlfriend from Chicago. I had been intimate with her when I was eighteen years old. I had always liked her. She was smart, athletic and full of fun. Now she was also a student at the U of I. She invited me to the house she shared with another young lady that had gone home for the weekend. My friend, I'll call her "Jane," did her best to entertain me with pictures and jokes but for some reason, I was uptight. Finally, "Jane" asked if something was bothering me. I confessed that I'd heard she was gay. She did not deny it. I've never been critical of homosexuals but in this case, it disconcerted me. My attitude ended what could have been a happy reunion. I wish I had handled it better.

The division of Special Services for War Veterans allowed a greater flexibility in choosing subjects to study. I specialized in business courses but also took courses in history, literature, and philosophy. I burned the midnight oil only when I had an important exam the next day, so I had a good amount of free time. When a friend who was a Sigma Nu "fraternity brother" urged me to join, and said I could have a meal job, I decided to "give it a shot." I did not stay long. I quit during "Hell Night" because of the silly and humiliating things pledges were subject to; when told I had to be the ping pong ball and jump back and forth over the net while being hit on the rump with a paddle, I walked off.

Just before "Hell Night," I took part in a juvenile prank. Pledges were regimented by the pledge masters and it was customary for pledges to retaliate eventually for the harsh treatment. On Fridays, most of the "actives" drove home after classes. Those that remain stayed in the dining room after dinner while the pledges forced the pledge master into the shower, clothes and all. Instead of putting our tormentor in the shower, we took him out the back way into a "getaway car." Two of the pledges had decommissioned the distributors in certain members' cars and thrown some mattresses and personal items outside. There were five or six of us and we drove to Kankakee, IL with the intention of keeping our captive prisoner until he missed his exam the following morning. After stopping for a beer, we arrived in Kankakee at a tavern that was also a "cathouse." I don't remember who suggested going there; only two of us were older than eighteen and we only found out later that it was a house of ill repute: the young'uns were in charge!

When two or three of the pledges went into the back room, a loud argument was heard and both bartenders came over the bar to handle the situation. I reacted without thinking and punched one of the bartenders. As he fell to the floor, I was hit from behind in the back of the neck, probably with a chair. I was on all fours on the floor while the others were hustled out the front. I tried to follow but five or six guys, probably customers, were determined to stop me. They surrounded me, trying to land punches but they got in each other's way and seemed afraid to get too close. I kept turning to prevent being jumped from behind. As I got closer to the front door, the would-be tough guys seemed more determined to stop me. I decided to take a punch and fall to the floor, thinking I would then simply be hustled out with the others. If I had been thinking clearly, I would have known better. As I crawled to the door I was kicked and hit with unknown objects, but I made it outside surprisingly intact.

The others were trying to defend against the bouncers and one of the kids asked a cop walking by for help. He was ignored. Either we held our own or the bouncers took it easy on us and we were able to get away. No one was badly hurt. My sweater was bloody and shredded, but I was okay. Since we all had fought together there was a mutual "esprit de corps" feeling and we returned our captive in time for his exam.

Back at the frat house, the actives were thrilled with our performance and they spread the word what great pledges we were. I was a little embarrassed by it all.

After final exams, I left on a trip to Mexico with Charlie. I did not wait to get all my grades but was confident that I had qualified for graduating. I did not need the credentials to get a job, as I had a job waiting with my father's company. From my teen years, I had secured sales outlets and sold merchandise for my dad's company.

It was not until three years after leaving school that I knew for sure that I had graduated. A woman phoned soliciting new members for the Illinois Alumni Association. I agreed to join, if she would have my diploma forwarded to me. Shortly thereafter I received a handsomely bound diploma from the Illinois University Division of Special Services for War Veterans.

Charlie and I boarded the train for Mexico City after storing my car in Laredo, Texas. The first stop was Monterey where we got coffee and snacks from women on the station platform. From there on the passenger car was filled with some men in suits, peasants, chickens and even a goat. A friendly Mexican gentleman initiated a conversation with us. He spoke excellent English and when we arrived at Mexico City, he invited us to have dinner at his home with he and his wife. We were happy to accept the invitation and were treated to an excellent meal. His wife did not speak English, but she was very friendly. Their villa was small but very pleasant and tastefully furnished.

Later that Sunday, our host took us to the bullfights. The bulls were fearless adversaries. It was considered necessary for picadors, mounted on horses, to use long lances to pierce and weaken the bulls neck muscles to lessen the dangers to the matador later. The picadors and their horses were protected with thick padding. Still it was a dangerous job. Sometimes horses were tumbled and the rider injured. We witnessed such an occasion. After badly injuring a horse and later killed by the matador's sword, the bull was dragged around the area by mules while the crowd chanted, "Ole." Afterwards, our host took us to the hotel he recommended; the Hotel Cadillac. We thanked him for his gracious hospitality and Charlie wrote his name and address down to mail a report on the trip. It had been a great day and it set the stage for relating with Mexicans which would be always favorable.

Hotel Cadillac was a first-rate hotel in the downtown area. Today it would be rated five stars. Surprisingly, the desk clerk did not speak English. That was okay with me. I wanted to try my limited

Spanish vocabulary. We got what I asked for, a room with two beds and a bath. I don't remember the cost but nothing we purchased in Mexico was costly. The exchange rate then was twelve pesos for a dollar. Twelve pesos would pay for three rooms in a modest hotel for Mexicans in Acapulco.

The young women we met in cantinas and elsewhere were friendly and sometimes initiated conversation. Apparently, they did not often see blond haired men as some would laugh and call me, "Blondie." We particularly enjoyed the Mariachi bands and the several days we spent in the capitol were very enjoyable. From there we took a wild bus ride through the mountains to Acapulco. The hotel we chose in Acapulco was used almost exclusively by Mexicans. We paid just 35 cents American money for the room. It was a good size and clean. A large ceiling fan supplied the air conditioning and our wall along the hallway was largely a venetian-type blind. The washroom was at the end of the hallway. We saved money on the room to pay for food, beer (cervesa) and fishing. Money that my mother had slipped into my luggage was a nice surprise. Both Charlie and I caught sailfish. We were lucky. The Mexican fisherman we hired had only a small boat and he would not go very far out into the ocean or stay out very long. Of course, the charge was a small fraction of what a regular charter boat would cost.

Charlie took the first turn fishing. Only one could troll at a time. He hooked a sail rather soon, but it took forty minutes to land it.

Sailfish caught by Bob in Acapulco 1955

As soon as the fish was in the boat, the captain headed for shore. He was pleased with the days results. Two days later we visited a beach used by wealthy tourists. I suggested to a young man there with girl friends that they might enjoy fishing on a charter boat. He agreed and engaged a boat and all of us boarded and set off. I was showing the young man how to use the rod and reel when fins from a group of sailfish broke the water just behind the boat. Our host failed to act to my urging him to cast the lure out, so finally I grabbed the rod and did it myself. Immediately a sail took the bait and I set the hook. A true sportsman might play the fish, but I horsed it in. A crewman used a gaff to land it. The fish measured 9.5 feet from the tip of his bill to the tail. Both fish were left with the boat captain after we took photos. Sailfish are considered excellent table fare when either broiled or smoked.

It was time to head home after a great vacation devoid of any unpleasantry or regret. Charlie and I parted at Laredo, as I was expected to work East Texas for the sale of postage stamp vending machines. I worked Texas for several weeks before going home to attend my sister Mary's wedding. My sales efforts were quite successful. I mostly called on those that had returned a reply card for info on the vending machines. Many of them presumed or hoped that the U.S. Post Office provided the machine free of charge. Actually, the cost was $79.00, quite a large sum in 1955. However, the economy was good and maybe I was good at selling. Later, after Mariann and I were married, she said it was because I looked like a choirboy. The machines proved to be a significant asset in most cases.

I worked diligently and tried to see everyone that was interested. One night I waited until after 9 PM for the owner of an outdoor produce market to return from Michigan. When he arrived, he bought two machines. Another time, I drove a long way over dirt roads before coming to a river with a self-operating ferry. It was necessary to drive onto a raft and pull it across the river with the rope and pulley system. It was a brief moment experiencing the life of a pioneer and I sold the machine to boot!

The Texans I called on were friendly, but I quickly learned to talk slowly and dress plainly. Some were cautious and took their time sizing me up. A few looked out the window to check my license plate, but the majority bought the deal.

Many of the small towns lacked something for a traveling

salesman to do in the evening. Televisions sets were not yet in common use. The Mexican border towns were something else. One night I walked across the Rio Grande bridge below McAllen, Texas into Reynosa, Mexico. I wandered into what I learned was called "Boys Town." There was a lot of activity, music, dancing and gaiety. I went into a cantina and ordered a beer. An attractive young woman asked if I wanted to dance. While we were dancing, a young man came and grabbed my partner's arm, threatening her with a knife while berating her furiously. To my surprise, she responded in kind and he abruptly walked away. We danced a few more times between drinks and later we had chili in the kitchen. It was getting dark when I left, and she walked with me to the Rio Grande bridge and even paid the 25 cents fee to cross. I regretted having to leave. Maybe I was getting ripe for marriage. I was almost 28 years old.

My sister, Mary, developed into an attractive, multitalented young woman. As a young girl, she took voice lessons, ballet and tap dancing and acrobatics. She developed a beautiful singing voice and played the piano well.

In 1955 Mary married Tom Duerr, a mechanical engineer from Ohio. Tom was hired by the U.S. government to participate in the Space Program centered in Huntsville, Alabama where he and Mary moved shortly after they were married. When Tom retired many years later, he did consulting work in the U.S. and Israel. Mary and Tom raised six children in Huntsville. They are all doing well. Mary and

All's Well

Tom still speak without a trace of a Southern accent but all their offspring sound quite Southern.

Courtship and Marriage

After coming home from Texas for Mary's wedding, I was sent to South Dakota on business. I came home for Thanksgiving and duck hunting with my brother Bill. We got home in the wee hours and Mom interrupted our sleep to have us meet someone. It was Mariann Stilwell who had been dating our brother Dick periodically for three years. Dick was playing on the Notre Dame football team and hoped to get together with Mariann over the holidays.

Mom had met Mariann at church in the morning and prevailed on her to stop at our house to "see Bill's kids." Mariann was somewhat reluctant but came anyway. Bill's kids weren't there; maybe Mom had expected Bill's wife, Barb, to come with the kids. Having been abruptly awakened, I went to the living room in a somewhat groggy state to find Mariann there. Neither of us realized that Mom was engaged in matchmaking. I was 27 years old and Mariann was 20 at the time.

After a short visit, I took Mariann home and asked if she would like to go rabbit hunting with me the following week. She said yes and I asked her to be ready at six a.m. Mariann was popular, attractive and proper. I was not popular and not yet proper. If I had been proper, I wouldn't have been out so late the night before and so late arriving at Mariann's the next day. She too had been out the night before but was ready at six a.m. My conduct might have ended our relationship but Mariann was intrigued. She had never been asked to go hunting before.

The hunt proved to be important for continuing the relationship. I shot a rabbit and then called in some crows. I shot two crows and hung them in a tree using them for decoys and more action. I am not sure that Mariann was impressed and I suggested she drive my new car while I looked for crows. I had assumed that Mariann knew how to drive. She promptly made too sharp a turn, going too fast and hit a concrete abutment, wrecking the car. It had to be towed back to Chicago for repairs. We took a train.

While waiting for repairs to be completed, I spent hours each day with Mariann who was recovering from flu like symptoms. I brought gifts including a cork gun and shooting gallery, records and rescuing a very skimpy family Christmas tree by drilling and filling it in with healthy boughs.

When the car was ready, I returned to South Dakota on

business. On December 23rd I received a note from momma matchmaker stating that Mariann with her young troop of cousins would be caroling at the house Christmas Eve. I drove the 625 miles over ice patches the next day. There was no interstate system yet. Providentially, I arrived at our house just as Mariann was leaving with her troop. We all had cocoa at her house and then I drove everyone home. We agreed to celebrate New Year's Eve together. Could it be that Mariann felt obligated having wrecked my car? OR was I actually a good salesman?

After New Year's Day we got together every Friday. Soon I asked Mariann to marry me. She seemed to be almost terrified at the thought, so in jest I said I would only ask again on Fridays. Several weeks later, as we were about to leave the house for a movie, I exclaimed "Hey, this is Friday! Mariann, will you marry me?" Mariann seemed almost panicked again but stammered, "Yes." It was February, Friday the 13th. After a hug and kiss, I rushed Mariann into the living room and gave our parents the news. I then asked, "Aren't you going to ask when?" I told them we would marry the coming May. It was also news to Mariann.

We were married May 26, 1956 at St. Gregory Catholic Church in Chicago. Mariann was gorgeous in a lovely wedding gown with veil and train borrowed from my sister. Mariann's cousin, Nancy Martin, was a bridesmaid and Aimee Thompson, maid of honor. Mariann and Aimee met as students of Webster College in St. Louis. Aimee was

Mariann and Bob
5-26-1956

from Huntsville, Alabama where Mariann and I live at this writing.

Mariann's Recollections: *At the Bachelor Dinner, Dick said I looked like hell. Little did I know I was incubating the measles virus caught from Aimee, my maid of honor. She had been exposed visiting a distant cousin prior to the wedding. I was terrified on our wedding day—a very big step after a very brief courtship. I could barely get out the "I Do." My cousin Larry, an usher, later said he thought he was going to have to throw a body block.*

Our first stop on the honeymoon was called "Heaven City" near Mukwonago, Wisconsin. It was a small resort with a cluster of quaint cottages set in a grove of apple trees loaded with blossoms. There was a small lounge and dining room. We had the dining room to ourselves that night. It had a stone floor with a large tree growing through the glass ceiling. A great dinner capped off the day.

The next day we drove to Madison, Wisconsin and a hotel on Lake Mendota. We had reservations made for us by brother Bill. Mariann was beginning to feel ill. We did not stay long before moving on toward Minnesota and Bowstring Lake. On the way, Mariann was examined by a doctor who thought it very funny that she had measles on her honeymoon. Maybe he thought that "Laughter is the Best Medicine," the title of the book by Art Linkletter. It did not work in this case.

On our arrival at Max, Minnesota and Bowstring Lake, we rented a cabin for a week. Mariann recalls: *The cabin had spiders the size of quarters and the oil stove blew up the first night. I was miserable with fever and headache and spent most of the time in bed. When I finally felt good enough to go fishing, Bob bundled me up in his G.I. clothing except that I wore shorts; determined to get a tan on my legs. We weren't out very long before my teeth were chattering, and I was freezing. Through clenched teeth Bob said, "You can't be cold." It turned out that I had sun poisoning due to the measles. Ran a fever for two days and my thighs swelled and blistered twice before peeling. What a honeymoon!*

By the time we returned to Chicago, Mariann had recovered and we set out on a yearlong trip across the country. It was a sales trip for me and a sight-seeing for both of us. We spent some time in Denver where Aimee lived and worked teaching in the elementary grades. I worked the area while the girls visited. We saw some of the local sights and moved on to Seattle where we had only a dime between us. Several thousand dollars were due me on sales, but we did not take the time to find a Western Union office and then wait for a money wire. Regular credit cards were not generally available yet and I hadn't tried to cash a check. I solved the problem by offering customers a cash discount for a cash deposit on the order; explaining why I wanted cash. We had plenty of cash from then on and the discount helped close sales.

We visited many of the national parks. At that time, they were not crowded. We did not see more than a dozen cars in Glacier

National Park and that was the norm.

Our last business trip was to Florida. We went out in a burst of glory. I sold 124 machines on that trip and Mariann got pregnant with Patrick. Back in Chicago we rented a small apartment on the far north side near the lake. Pat was born 8/31/57 the same day as his mother—8/31/35. He was three weeks premature and weighed 7 lbs. 4 oz, but he ate like a horse and gained weight fast. Mariann was losing weight and could not keep up with Pat's voracious appetite. We soon were feeding him cereal and baby food. He was a frantic eater, red-faced, with his little hands thrashing furiously between us, as we tried to get the spoon into his mouth before he could knock it away. When his initial hunger pains subsided, he regained his normal color and relaxed.

In 1957 it did not take long to drive from our apartment to the office of Fitzgerald Associates, in downtown Chicago. Our office was located in the Fairbanks Morse building on Michigan Avenue overlooking Buckingham Fountain and a beautiful view of Grant Park and Lake Michigan. My brother Bill was helping our father appoint distributors for Regiscope, a new product. Regiscope was a dual-lens camera used to photograph simultaneously a check and the person cashing the check. The photo was important for identifying the maker, if the check bounced. When distributor appointments were proceeding nicely, our dad relinquished control and Bill took over independent of Fitzgerald Associates. Before long, a problem with the camera's function led to a lawsuit against the manufacturer. Bill left and took a position in California with a swimming pool company. It became necessary for Fitzgerald Associates to also sue Regiscope Mfg. for commissions due.

The lawsuit was adjudicated in the superior court, downtown Chicago by a prominent judge. The manufacturing company was represented by three lawyers from California. After hearing both sides, the judge said he would hear the summations in his chambers. Our lawyer surprised Dad and I by asking me to give the summation. Perhaps he hadn't reviewed the case sufficiently. I gave the summation. A law student that I roomed with during my first year at the University of Illinois said I should be studying to be a lawyer. I am pretty sure, however, that my summation had little to do with the outcome of the trial. The verdict was for Fitzgerald Associates. In the hall, while leaving, the opposing lawyers said we shouldn't have won. I hope they did not think we won because the judge's name was also Fitzgerald.

Bill and his family hadn't been in California long when his new employer went bankrupt. After a long, persistent endeavor, Bill was able to form a new company endorsed by Art Linkletter, TV host and author of "Kids Say the Darndest Things" and Hal Totten, celebrated dance master. Bill then secured investor owners for Linkletter-Totten Schools of Dance on a national basis.

Bill's next endeavor was developing his own mailing company for securing inquiries for others. Finally, Bill traveled the country buying campgrounds for a well-funded company until he retired to Florida with his wife Colleen. Bill died of natural causes in 2017 at the age of 90. We all miss "Beau Brummel."

When I quit the road in 1957, the company income from the sale of stamp machines fell sharply. We began looking for another product and learned that "hangover" pills were selling well in Texas. After some checking we began testing the local sale of hangover pills together with other remedies; 2–4 pills, packaged in heat-sealed aperture packets of several products were displayed on store counters. Results were encouraging and we selected four best sellers to merchandise with impressive display racks. After further testing, we were ready to appoint distributors. A partner met with the sales manager of Plough Brothers who said that the booklet I authored entitled the "Pac Aid Story" was one of the best pieces of promotional literature he had seen. The introduction of "Pac Aids" took place in Detroit. We supplied free displays with several packets of each product to selected retailers. The promotion was backed by TV coverage and a press conference. We thought the Pac Aid business was on its way to success when we received a serious setback. A letter from the Federal Drug Administration challenged the copy on the packets.

We had been careful to use only accepted language on the packets so that was a big surprise. We consulted a reputable firm of attorneys specializing in drug related cases. They advised that it would take a lot of time and money to fight the claim and we would probably lose. Whether they were right or not, we could not afford to persist. I should have heeded Mariann's opinion when I first thought of Pac Aids. Having worked for a top executive in a leading drug manufacturing company in Chicago, Mariann feared that the "big boys" in the business would likely try to shut us down. We abandoned Pac Aids. Dad and I flew to Detroit hoping to make another connection there. The conference with a potential associate was prolonged and unsuccessful. We missed our flight back to Chicago and waited for the next one. There was a lot of turbulence over O'Hare and we were in a holding pattern for several minutes. After landing safely, we learned that the flight we missed went down in Lake Michigan with no survivors.

In 1959, Mariann and I bought a house on contract in the Chicago northwest suburbs. Fitzgerald Associates was no longer in business. Dad took a position as traveling editor for a book publisher. The book was published annually and listed important people in the scientific field that had died. Dad interviewed the families of the deceased, securing the desired information and discussing options for featuring the subject with an illustration in the coming issue.

Meanwhile, I had designed an improved type postage stamp vending machine and was seeking an association with a manufacturer for its production. The machine would be capable of dispensing from one to five stamps from one roll, and if desired, from one to five stamps from a second roll at the same time; one customer operation. This flexibility would enable the machine to handle postage rate changes; unlike other stamp vending machines. By use of standard coin mechanisms, different coins could be used.

Our next-door neighbor introduced me to two brothers owning a manufacturing plant that was ideal. We reached an agreement for a partnership where they invested $25,000 for machine production with Dad and I contributing the sales organization and the machine design. Our partners had fifty some presses and a tool room with ten tool and die makers. I worked with one of them to produce a working model. Permanent dies were then made and production of the Selectra machines began in about six months' time. In a short time Selectra machines became the leaders in the field and the U.S. Postal Service requested a few of the slide-out mechanisms for testing. They were planning to field-test self-service stations for postage stamp sales. The Selectra mechanisms performed well in laboratory tests using dummy stamp rolls. We were then asked to produce special larger sized machines. I presented the first of these during a ceremony in the Rotunda of the U.S. Capitol Building. Months later, the postal service abandoned the self-service plan for outdoor postage stamp sales. Still, the publicity and prestige from our association with the U.S. Postal Service was very beneficial for Selectra Inc. We sold many machines thereafter to Sears, Wards, Walgreens and many supermarket chain stores. More than 30,000 Selectra units were sold. Eventually, I received U.S. Patents on the Selectra design and two other products. One was a multiproduct vending machine and the other, a unique display rack.

Bob presenting machine in the Rotunda of the Capitol, Washington, D.C.

Our Cuban

Back Row: Mariann, Shan, Henry, Bob
Front Row: Mike, Pat, Katie

February 1962, Pat was now four and a half years old, Shannon, 3 years old, Mike almost 2 years old, and Katie, just a baby. Mariann and I had joined the "Christian Family Movement," an action organization for helping needy families. I was group leader when it was announced in church that there was a need for families willing to take in Cuban children sent to other countries to escape Castro's communism. It was to be temporary, only until the parents were able to also come. Mariann and I volunteered.

Henry, our Cuban, was 15 years old at the time. He was quite good looking and spoke some English. Henry's father had been vice treasurer under Batista, Henry's mother was from an aristocratic family. They had separated and did not intend to leave Cuba.

Henry had been raised by servants and was quite spoiled—a mama's boy. We enrolled him at St. Viators High School just two blocks from our house. It took a while for Henry to accept direction from his teachers and he persisted, for a while, in scaring the little kids. He would threaten to put them in the oven or the washing machine. One day when I arrived home early, I caught Henry outside holding Pat headfirst in the trash can. When he saw me, he bolted, but I caught him and dragged him back to the trash can and put him in— also headfirst. Henry was incredulous that an old man of 35 could catch him. The next day he challenged me to a foot race which he lost. Henry was not athletic. Next, he challenged me to a swimming contest—he knew I had a bad shoulder. We raced at the community pool. I swam side stroke and Henry lost again. It helped deflate his arrogance. Henry's conduct improved but he still frightened the kids sometimes. One morning we found Shannon sleeping on the floor at the foot of our bed. Mariann's mother and her aunt often spent weekends with us but soon quit coming. They were angry because we did not send Henry back to Catholic Charities.

Sometime later, Mariann was in bed sick and Henry refused to watch the kids. Mariann then asked me to take Henry back to Catholic Charities in Chicago. Henry became quite angry when I told him to pack—he tried to leave on a bike. When restrained he said, "One of us is going to get hurt Bob." He weighed about 130 pounds and I over 200 pounds. I have to give him credit for self-esteem.

After I brought Henry back to Catholic Charities office, he was assigned to other families, but none would keep him for long. Eventually he came back to talk to Mariann. She told him to talk to me. I told Henry it had been much better for all of us since he left. He laughed. His good-natured reaction was a surprise and it helped me decide to give him another chance. Henry got a job at a local supermarket and he stayed with it. When his father phoned from Miami, Mariann invited him for Christmas. Henry's father replied that it was too cold for him in Illinois. As Mariann said afterward, "That explains Henry's attitude." Henry's older brother, William, had lived with his father in Cuba and Henry with his mother after the parents' separation. William had an important position with our government in Washington, D.C. He had a bodyguard, according to Henry. William's wife was a microbiologist. They had no children. I assume the father went to D.C.

Following Mariann's invitation, William came to visit us and Henry. He was polite and spoke good English. Henry said his brother was dull, simple-minded and did not even know *where* the airport was in D.C. In reality, William was very intelligent. He had received a full scholarship at the Catholic University in Washington, D.C.

Henry eventually earned a master's degree in business administration from Loyola University in Chicago. He is ambitious and aggressive and became an expert at commercial real estate appraising. Henry also served several times as an expert witness in court. At this writing, Henry is 71 years old, married, without children and a multimillionaire. He lives in a Chicago suburb and phones Mariann often. Henry considers us family.

Adventures in Home and Hunting

During the prosperous years, we bought a beautiful piece of land still further north of Chicago and about ten miles from the Wisconsin state line. It consisted of 21 acres at the back end of a small, wooded subdivision. There were ten, one acre lots in the subdivision. We bought one of the lots for access to the twenty-acre parcel in back. About five acres at the front of the twenty-acre parcel were high and had many large oak and hickory trees. From these five acres, it sloped down to a ten- or eleven-acre peat bog with another five or six acres of high ground to the side.

We were all eager to move to the property as soon as possible. Living there would add close to an hour to the commute to the office but weekends alone at Timber Trail made it more than worthwhile. On weekends we all worked together planting trees and shrubs on the high ground in the back of the property. I dug the holes; even Mariann was not big enough to force the trenching spade deep into the soil. The kids all did their part. Mike filled water pails from the well hole I dug in the marsh. Shannon and Pat carried the water to the planting areas. Katie gathered peat to mix with the dirt backfill for plantings. She was only six years old and quickly grew tired of her job. She was heard to say at breakfast one morning, "I hope this isn't a peat moss day!" It was and it would be for some time to come. We expected a lot from our kids, and they grew up to be strong and able.

Bob on utility tractor at Timber Trail homestead

During this period, Henry, our Cuban, was living in Chicago, managing a key club and studying at Loyola U for a degree in business. He visited us often, sometimes with girlfriends. Henry liked to hunt but had little patience. We were hunting pheasants once in a picked cornfield. After only five minutes or so without seeing any pheasants, Henry exclaimed, "This is no fun" and returned to the truck where he waited for about twenty minutes. He was surprised when I returned with two cock pheasants. Sometime later, Henry came along when Mariann and I visited friends in central Illinois. We were sitting at the bar in town with a man that had been in a German POW camp during World War II. Recognizing Henry as a foreigner, the man asked me what we fed him. Thinking he was kidding, I responded "Bananas and coconuts." The man nodded, satisfied and I realized he hadn't been kidding. Henry still laughs about it. We haven't seen Henry since before we moved to Alabama, but he calls to talk with Mariann often.

I bought my first bow to practice archery while still living in the suburbs. It was a recurve bow; compound bows were not yet popular. One day I shot a practice arrow with a field point at a rabbit feeding on our tulips. It was a distance of about twenty yards, and I shot from inside the kitchen with the door ajar. The rabbit ran out of our yard, but I could not find the arrow. The next day, Pat said he'd seen a rabbit and arrow in the next-door neighbor's trashcan. It was embarrassing. I found my arrow sticking through the top of the rabbit's skull. Fortunately, I was undetected as I removed the rabbit and arrow. It was a good shot with a not so good result as far as others might think.

All's Well

Later, when we were living on a farm prior to building the new house, I bought a compound bow. After a lot of practice, I was able to shoot accurately. I never have used a mechanical release and remain a finger shooter, with the bow set at a seventy-pound draw. The adjacent farm, where I had permission to hunt had a ten-acre woodlot at the road separated from a ninety-acre woods by a small meadow. A large whitetail buck deer used the ten-acre woodlot for bedding. On three occasions I was within fifty feet of the buck while bowhunting. I wore camouflage, body scent suppressor and a facemask. Most importantly, I tried to stay downwind of my quarry. The first time I was close to the buck was when I had the family walk through the ten-acre bedding area while I perched in a tree at the far corner. I heard the buck coming through the dry leaves, but he emerged behind me in the meadow. I was unable to turn around while the buck stood at attention. When I shot, the fiberglass arrow shattered in midair. I hadn't yet realized that the arrow initially flies higher than the line of sight and it hit the drooping end of a branch.

The buck escaped and I learned not to use glass arrows for hunting and that the arrow flies higher than the line of sight when released. I also learned that perching in a tree limits the direction in which you will be able to shoot. The next time I encountered this buck, I was crouching behind a thick hedge at the opposite side of the meadow. As the light began to fade that evening, I saw the buck approaching cautiously through the meadow along the hedge. I was waiting about ten yards from a trail through the hedge leading into the cornfield behind me. He came down slowly through the hedge and stopped when only his head and neck was exposed. He studied the field and I began to slowly draw back the arrow on the string. The buck looked my way and I could not hold steady long enough. My hand started shaking and the buck spun around and disappeared. I shouldn't have drawn the bowstring till he was well into the field. The last chance I had at that buck; I was ten feet up in a tree in the hedge but closer to the big woods. This time the buck was within twenty yards when I shot the arrow. He shrieked and went down on his knees but bounced right back up and ran into the woods. I thought he would lay down soon and die, if I did not pursue too quickly. I went to the house and waited. An hour later, I searched the woods with a flashlight for over an hour and found nothing. The next morning, I searched again and found only a part of the arrow where the buck had been hit. Several days later at a local convenience store the sheriff approached and said he wanted to show me something. I followed to his garage where two beautiful bucks were hanging from the rafters. He handed over my broadhead he took from one of the bucks while butchering it. I suspect he had "shined" both deer from the road at night and shot them with a rifle. Deer usually stand motionless when shined at night. Hunting after dark, shining game, using a rifle and taking more than one buck was all illegal; but he was the sheriff.

It was very frustrating and another learning experience for me.

I should not have aimed at the shoulder but rather behind the shoulder where the heart and other vital organs are located. Eventually, I would learn enough from the mistakes to harvest a number of deer.

Pat was almost seven years old when we bought the twenty-one acres. Like his mother, Pat was a "people person" motivated to relate well with others. However, when I learned he was content with being tied to a tree and shot with rubber tipped arrows by a neighbor boy I urged him to be more aggressive and defend himself. He could do fifty pushups and was very able. He countered with, "But Dad, I want to play with him."

We decided that I should take Pat camping on our property for a meeting of the minds. Good weather was predicted for the weekend, so we gathered the necessary food, clothing, fishing gear, shotgun, pup tent and other items. Fortunately, I had a lot of camping experience from canoe trips taken years earlier. On the way to the property we stopped at a trout farm and caught a couple of rainbows for dinner. After erecting the tent, I cut and split enough wood for cooking and a lot of time around the campfire. I related stories about hunting and fishing and told Pat how the love of the outdoors had enriched my life. Pat was enjoying the experience and looking forward to hunting ducks in the morning.

After breakfast, we walked in the dark to the back of the property. There was no lake there yet, but I cleared a small area of rushes for open water in the marsh. At dawn, I shot two ducks that came into land. We had been hiding in the tall grass close by. The success so early was gratifying but my enthusiasm lessened when I retrieved the ducks. They were mergansers, fish ducks, and poor table fare, but I did not mention that to Pat. After lunch, we explored the area before heading home. The camp out had been a success.

By the time Pat was in seventh grade, he had changed radically. He was reading at a college level and was strong and confident. Girls in his classroom looked to him for protection from the bullies. Shannon said that Pat was their hero.

Before building our home on the property, we moved to a farmhouse near the Wisconsin state line and had an architect draw plans for the house to be built on the twenty-one-acre property. It would be a cedar-sided ranch built on the downslope of the hill overlooking the back of the property and the farmland beyond. The lower level would have three bedrooms and a recreation room, all with sliding glass doors to the outside. The upper level would have the master bedroom, kitchen and the fifty-foot-long dining-living room combination. There would be a mudroom closet with a half-bath between the kitchen and garage. All rooms would have sliding glass doors.

At the end of the farmhouse lease, the new house was not yet ready. The grandparents took the kids and Mariann and I roughed it for a few weeks lacking water, septic and electricity. We trucked water from neighboring houses, used oil lamps, Weber grill and the washroom in the nearby service station. It was an ordeal: our furniture, belongings and miscellany sharing space with lumber, saws and workmen going in and out.

When the new house was ready, my father brought everyone out to see it. We had a picnic there. Mariann and I were sitting on lawn chairs, along with her mom and aunt, and a couple from Germany with their ten-year-old boy. They owned two of the front acres adjoining our property. Gerd owned a beauty salon in a suburb north of Chicago. It was a very exclusive shop catering to wealthy women that he referred to in a negative way. They had their oversized dachshund along with them and the boy was throwing a tennis ball for their dog to retrieve. Tuck wanted to compete, so we leashed him to a small tree trunk close by. Suddenly Tuck broke loose and got to the ball first. The doxy bit Tuck in the rear as Tuck was picking up the ball. Tuck whirled around and grabbed the doxy by the back, lifting it off the ground. Maybe it was the screaming of Gerd's wife and relatives but maybe I hadn't yet taught Tuck the "drop it" command. But I grabbed Tuck by his collar and the base of his tail and lifted both dogs off the ground, shaking them both. For some strange reason, Gerd was beaming. I realized I was doing the wrong thing and put the dogs down. At my urging, Tuck released the doxy and it ran off. The once bold dog was found hiding under a car and it had bloody holes in its sides. The next time the couple came out to the property, the woman handed me the vet's bill for the doxy's treatment. Gerd said it had been hit by a car and died. I wondered.

After a few years, we had a large inground swimming pool installed. I built a redwood deck with a cabinet for pool tools and supplies. Later, a regulation size tennis court was put in and I fenced the court with 4x4 posts and green coated wire mesh. If a tennis ball was hit into the woods, one of the Labs would fetch it.

I bought a Ford utility tractor with hydraulic lift for attaching a mower, plow, carry-all or other implements. A tractor shed served also for storage and a workshop. We raised mallard ducks from eggs in our incubator in the dining room and pheasants from chicks. The mallards were laying the eggs in the water and I daily went down to the pond to retrieve them; releasing them when mature. The pheasants' beak tips were clipped off to prevent them from pecking each other when penned. The chicks were kept in chicken wire enclosures to protect them from mink, weasels, hawks and other predators.

Every spring for the first several years, we had a huge dragline dig in the slough until we had a six-acre lake. In Illinois a six or more-acre body of water is classified as a lake. The water depth exceeded ten feet in places, and we planted cedar trees on the islands. The dragline had a one cubic yard bucket attached to cables that could be thrown out over fifty feet. The bucket was dragged back gathering soil. The contents of the bucket were deposited to the rear.

The dragline had to sit on "pads" made up of huge oak timbers lashed together with cables. To move, the boom hooked a second pad laying behind the dragline and placed it in front. With its two-foot-wide tracts, the dragline could then move forward onto the second pad leaving the first pad behind. Without the pads, the dragline would have sunk into the soft soil.

The lake was stocked with bass, bluegill, channel catfish and sometimes rainbow trout. All but the trout propagated in the lake. Trout require cold, moving water to thrive and reproduce. The boys and I took the pickup truck to buy minnows in Wisconsin. On the way home, Pat and Mike kept the 80-gallon tank aerated by dipping out water and splashing it back into the tank. It is important to keep certain minnows out of ponds. Carp and other "rough" fish can muddy the waters and eat the spawn of game fish. We also had good luck fishing.

For many years, we always had at least one Labrador retriever, the most popular breed in the U.S. They are intelligent, friendly, aim to please and love kids. Labs are great swimmers and famous for use in hunting ducks. At the time, they were not often used for upland bird hunting, like pheasant hunting. However, I trained our Labs to obey whistle and hand signals and to work close and within gunshot range when hunting pheasants. Today Labrador retrievers are used extensively for locating objects by scent. Their superior scenting ability was known to our family long ago. Frequently, I would have Mariann release one of our Labs after allowing me time to climb a tree hundreds of yards from the house. At the command, "Find Bob," the dog would run directly to me, catching my scent from the air above the ground. One time I ran along the lakeshore, dove in and swam to a shallow area with a lot of rushes. While in about four feet of water, surrounded by rushes, I could see our Lab, Tuck, racing down the hill from the house. He came to the spot where I had dived in and swam directly to me. I was not surprised. All our Labs found me every time I tried to hide from them.

Tuck was our first Lab. We bought him and a much larger female German shepherd when we moved from the suburbs to the farmhouse prior to building the new house on our twenty-one acres. The shepherd dominated the smaller Lab and would often nip at him, so we named them Nip and Tuck. All our dogs were always given one syllable names: Tuck, Beau, Gay and Buck. The first three were black Labs and the last two (Bucks) were yellow Labs. They all performed really well but Tuck was probably the best. He developed into the best watchdog and family protector, as well as a very enthusiastic hunting dog. As a young pup on the farm, he was bullied by Nip who made him wait to eat until she had enough, even though they had separate bowls. One day, Mariann heard a loud squealing coming from the porch. Looking out an upstairs window, she saw Tuck up on a bench, holding Nip by her nose. From then on, he was the boss.

Years later, a friend wanted to mate his female Lab with Tuck. We chose Beau from the litter and bought Gay from a man that trained hunting dogs for field trials. We had a concrete slab poured on which I erected chain link fencing for side by side kennels. Then I built a doghouse for each kennel; both with recessed compartments insulated by straw. These houses were adequate for our coldest weather and both the lower back and top could be opened for ventilation in the summer.

Gay and Beau were kept in the kennel and Tuck became the housedog because he was older and a great watchdog. Henry and another friend tried on different occasions to let themselves in the house while waiting for us. Tuck was too intimidating even though they knew his name and they stopped trying to get in the house while we were away.

Beau was the best tennis ball retriever. After a number of balls were hit into the woods, we sent Beau to get them. Often, he would bring three balls at a time in his mouth but try to give us only two until we insisted he give up the third. He was a fun dog.

Flying squirrels were discovered when I was cutting down a dead oak tree. The tree was hollow halfway up and a family of flying squirrels suddenly began gliding in all directions as I cut. It was a rare and awesome experience. The property had about every type of wildlife common to the Midwest, but I had never before seen flying squirrels.

One year, I bought several ducks with clipped wings that prevented them from flying. They were said to be "callers" for bringing in wild ducks. I put them in a small pond at the back of the property. The pond had been dug by a pipeline contractor that had cut down some of our young trees without permission. It was dug in settlement of our claim against him.

One foggy Sunday morning, I heard shots fired in the back. While Mariann was phoning the sheriff's office, I raced back there on the tractor. Two teenage boys were shooting the "callers." I demanded that they pay for the ducks they shot. They did not have the money even though I was charging only the amount I had paid. As they were leaving, a deputy called with a bullhorn for them to come to the road where *he* was waiting. I told the deputy that the boys would pay for the ducks and I did not plan on filing a complaint. I don't believe they were charged with a violation; probably because they were young.

The following spring, two brothers that were burning off grass in their field behind us lost control of the fire. We saw the smoke and flames from our hilltop house. Again, while Mariann phoned the fire department, I rushed to the back of our property with a pump and hose in the water tank on the tractor carrier. I also had a rag mop and a broom to spread water on the dry grass for a firebreak. The brothers helped although they were exhausted and teary eyed from fighting the fire.

We had it pretty well under control when the fire truck arrived. It was a close call, but I did not learn sufficiently from the experience because I had a grass fire of my own get out of control sometime later. On a Sunday morning when the grass was still damp, I was having difficulty getting it to burn. A little later I got it to burn but it soon got to be too much for one person to handle. Shannon came running from the house to help. Mariann had left. Shannon and I managed to save most of the evergreen trees nearby, but a ten-foot blue spruce went up in flames. I think I finally learned that it takes a lot of help to safely conduct a burn.

Another learning experience involved the septic system. Our system consisted of three leaching pits connected to the septic tank. The pits were about six feet deep, five feet wide, lined with porous blocks and filled with septic gravel. Eventually, the system failed, and effluent backed up into the house, twice. I rented equipment to ream out the four-inch drainpipes in the house by way of the septic tank. I emptied the septic tank with my trash pump and hose. Then, I decided to improve the system with a much bigger leaching pit at the backside of the house. With a scoop-like bucket on the tractor's three-point hitch, I dug a trench from the tank to the point where the hill sloped down to the woods below. Next, I hired an excavator to dig an eighteen-foot-deep hole at the end of the trench. The hole was then filled with pea gravel, and I finally disconnected the original drain tile from the septic tank and connected the new, perforated drain tile. The new drain tile extended from the tank through the trench and looped around the pea gravel until it covered it completely. The "fix" ended our problems with the septic system.

The whole family frequently joined in playing water volleyball. A rope was stretched down the center of the forty-foot length of the pool to serve as a net. Most of the pool was five to ten feet deep and there was a twelve-inch ledge around the deep area.

Many years later, before Mariann and I left the property, we hosted a block party. After hours of competition between the young people, two teenaged boys emerged as the champs. Shannon and I challenged them to a contest. Shan was a good competitor and I did okay using just one arm. I think the boys were surprised when an old, one armed man and a girl bested them in a hard-fought contest.

Tuck was getting up in years when he and Beau got into a terrible fight. A friend and I had just finished hunting on a neighbor's farm. The dogs were in the bed of the truck when the fight started. I quickly got into the back with the dogs, but it appeared unlikely that I could separate them without help. My friend was reluctant to help and stayed in the cab up front. Each dog had a neck hold on the other dog. The previous winter these two had gotten into a bad fight. Four of us family members together with a neighbor became exhausted trying to get the dogs apart. Finally, I connected a hose to a water spigot and held it to their noses until the water stream cut their breathing and they had to release their holds. Tuck was scooped up and put in the truck. The snow was bloody and disturbed but I found a fang of Tuck that the vet reattached later that night. The fang stayed put for the rest of Tuck's life.

Now I was facing the same dilemma without help. I was desperate and tried something radical. Grabbing the smaller Tuck, I was able to drop him over the closed tailgate. I thought Beau would have to let go but surprisingly he held on while Tuck was dangling in the air. Then, when Tuck whimpered, in desperation I commanded Beau to, "Drop it." He obeyed the command he had heard often in the past. What a relief! I rushed Tuck into the cab and examined him for injuries. This time it was not necessary to have the vet open his clinic on a Sunday.

One summer day, our first yellow Lab did something surprising. A cock pheasant flushed as Buck and I were walking down to the lake. It flew to the other end of the lake—over three hundred yards. Buck ran after it and I let him go. To my great surprise, Buck returned with the uninjured pheasant. I put the bird in a closed kennel for observation. When I checked back the pheasant was hiding behind the doghouse, so I went in and chased it out. The bird flew up into a large oak tree. With Buck nearby I scared it out of the tree, and it flew far into our neighbor's property. Our neighbor was known as the Marlboro Man, as seen in tv commercials. Len was a good guy. The back of his property was an overgrown wildlife haven. Len lived in a log cabin on the wooded hill at the front. The pheasant landed in thick cover. Buck was watching and ran after it. Soon I saw Buck emerge from the tall grass with the bird in his mouth. When Buck stopped to lift his leg and pee, the pheasant got away. Once again Buck disappeared into the high grass. When he reappeared, he had the pheasant and brought it to me. This time it was not in good condition and I processed it for the dinner table.

One day before Christmas, I took my shotgun and walked alone to the back of the property. I was shocked to find that the specimen, an eight-foot blue spruce I had planted years before, had been cut down. There were two sets of footprints and drag marks in the snow leading to a neighbor's property. I followed and after going through the hedge separating the properties, I saw two men together and one was dragging the tree. They were a couple hundred yards distant and about the same distance from their house on the next road north. I yelled but they ignored me, so I shot off a shell. They stopped and turned to me as I hurried toward them. Suddenly, one of them hurried to the house. I realized that he might be going for a gun, but I continued on. The thief was a "hunk" that had hooked up with the attractive gal that owned the property. I had confronted him the previous summer when he was fishing in our lake. I noted then that he seemed somewhat simple minded. Now, face to face, I vented my ire. His face turned red, probably from both anger and humiliation. He did not offer to make restitution or to return the tree. I told him he had twenty minutes to deliver the tree to my house, or I would call the sheriff. He then said he would bring the tree to the house and the next spring there would be an equally nice tree at my doorstep. The tree was returned in time but there was no replacement the next spring. I don't think he was even around the next spring. I think his "keeper" kicked him out.

Pat

Patrick "Pat" Fitzgerald

It was a wonderful time for all of us, but things were about to change. The kids were beginning to show their independent natures. They tried pot and liquor and acted irresponsibly at times. Mariann and I tried to guide them, but we knew it was common for teens to rebel. We felt we shouldn't be too righteous since we had faults of our own and we also used liquor often.

Our son, Pat, left unannounced when he was just sixteen years old. He hitchhiked to Florida and sent a letter saying he was okay. Initially, he slept on the beach and cooked over campfires. His first employer was a mover. Then he took a job dishwashing at a Denny's restaurant. After a while, he was offered the position there of manager. He was still only sixteen but looked and acted older. Pat turned down the offer and left after friends from Illinois arrived. Sometime later, Pat was arrested for taking some lunchmeat from a convenience store. When notified, we sent money for his release, after which he returned home. He had been away for several months. Pat's independent impulses continued to be a problem. He hitchhiked to Chicago soon after returning from Florida. In Chicago, he was picked up by the police for loitering and having no identification. I drove to Chicago and retrieved him from juvenile detention. We were relating well on the drive home but when I corrected him about something, he got out of the car at a stop sign and hitched a ride home.

Mariann and I thought it might help to enroll Pat at a Jesuit school in Wisconsin that had a reputation of success with adolescent boys. We drove there to make arrangements. When we advised Pat of our intentions, he rebelled and left unannounced to stay with a friend. We then consulted with a local psychologist with a reputation for relating well with teenagers. He directed us to a husband and wife team that operated a "home" in the country for troubled boys. Of course, we were also to have sessions with Pat and the counselor. The whole thing was costly but in spite of my skepticism, Mariann wanted to give it a try. The program was supposed to be temporary. There were eight other young men in the home. The boys were catered to and seemed quite content to be there. They were supposed to wear white blazers and dress slacks when dining at fancy restaurants and meetings with publicity agents for photos. One of the treatments included having the boys tested by a graphologist. We were then told that Pat was "scripted" to be a problem. I began to lose hope that their program could help Pat and brought him home.

Before Pat left the country "resort" for "problem boys" he hitchhiked to Fox Lake, a small town in northern Illinois where his favorite cousin lived. The cousin was a slight boy a year older who had been brutally beaten by a football player who had been harassing his sister. At his dad's insistence the cousin had had confronted the bully and had been beaten. He was afraid he and his sister would continue to be menaced and he asked for Pat's help. Pat cornered the bully and gave him a thrashing and a warning. We learned of it only from the cousin's mother. Pat had come full circle from a little boy that allowed himself to be tied to a tree and shot with arrows because he wanted a playmate to a tough warrior like personality. I hadn't tried to make him that way, maybe it was in the genes.

The following year, Pat was shot by a sheriff's deputy. The police said it was a "bad shooting," meaning it was a mistake. There hadn't been a lot of criminal activity around Crystal Lake, Illinois at that time, so a robbery of a convenience store clerk at knife point created a lot of excitement for law enforcement. It was "war games on Friday night."

They were looking for a Hispanic type young man. There was

an 11 p.m. curfew in effect for underage kids and Pat and his friends were heading home. While fooling around with his buddies in the dark, Pat ran into a telephone pole support cable and was injured. His friends went to call for help while Pat lay on the ground. The woman manager of a bowling alley on the outskirts of town refused the boys entrance and called the police. Pat had told his buddies not to call us, so they went to call for a friend with a car. While at the nearby phone booth, several police cars arrived. The new police chief brought from Chicago to "control the longhaired troublemakers" had strong arm tactics he used to make the boys tell where Pat was. A police photographer days later showed me photos of the battered boys.

The chief sent a single deputy to get Pat. Later that night the deputy admitted under oath that he had cursed Pat vilely and threatened to shoot him if he did not get on the ground. He said that Pat replied, "I am going to get you pig." The deputy said he meant to hit Pat with his flashlight but the look on Pat's face scared him and he shot him instead. The deputy, an ex-marine, stood 6'4", weighed about 240 lbs. and was said to be a karate expert. Pat was about 5'10" and weighed about 170 at the most. When I phoned the FBI's Chicago office, the agent I spoke with angrily defended the deputy. He said it is not easy to restrain yourself when attacked in a dark field. If Pat actually attacked the deputy, it still is odd that with the size difference and the deputy's qualifications that he would panic. *The deputy admitted under oath several times that Pat had no knife.* The real villains were the chief who sent a single tough guy to "get" Pat, the cop that planted the "cover up" knife and those that lied or stayed quiet too long.

A year or more later when the case against the police for the "bad shooting" was pending, a woman came to my office. She wanted $900 that she said was still owed her, although it was the first time I'd heard it mentioned. She insinuated that she could make it known that Pat was a problem kid. He was not a problem to others, but I gave her the $900 to get rid of her.

Two years later, we finally got hold of the "lost" transcript of the deputy's statement before the State's Attorney the night Pat was shot. A newly appointed official gave a copy to our lawyer, not realizing his error. The claim that Pat attacked the deputy with a knife was broadcast via TV and radio. It was on the front page of the Chicago newspapers. The police chief repeated the claim during radio and TV interviews and even in the schoolroom with our two younger children present. Mike stood up and told the chief that Pat did not carry a knife! The chief lied about a lab identifying the knife as Pat's. The knife being held as evidence was far too long to fit in the pockets of the cutoffs Pat was wearing. Pat died on the way to the hospital ten miles away almost an hour after being shot. We were called to come to the hospital about three hours after that.

Of course, our family was devastated. I made the mistake of accepting a neighbor's recommendation of a local lawyer. After conducting a number of interrogations, or interrogatories in lawyer's talk, he advised that our claim involved a federal court hearing and he was not prepared to travel to Chicago. We later learned that he also represented several of the police districts that took part in this tragedy. Two years later, a second lawyer well-meaning friends sent to see us took the case. He repeated all the interrogatories initially done. Then he met with the insurance claims officer and reported that the county was insured for only $35,000. He urged us to take it. He said otherwise it could be in court for years and we were in no shape emotionally. Mariann and I agreed even though we knew that the lawyer needed a chunk of money soon. It was also significant that the police chief had left the force soon after the shooting. The $35,000 was split almost equally between the lawyers and us. Then I was sued by the firm that transcribed the interrogatories for the second lawyer. When I related this to the first lawyer, of his own volition, he sent his young assistant to the court hearing. I lost probably because the lawyer that really owed the money was an Illinois State Legislator. Believing that the local lawyer would not charge me, I mailed $300 to him for his assistant's failed endeavors. I got a return bill from him for $700. He took me to small claims court because I refused to pay, and I lost the decision again. By now, I was plenty outraged and disillusioned with lawyers, judges and law enforcement.

Katie

Kathleen "Katie" Fitzgerald
Boulder, Colorado

Katie was the only one of our kids that took schoolwork seriously and she was on the honor roll through high school. She was not as agreeable as her sister, but she was a good girl. She was very independent and wanted things done her way, so Katie did not have a lot of friends. When her siblings wanted to pool their money for Christmas gifts for us, she refused to be part of it. She was stoic and disciplined. Neither Mariann nor I can remember Katie crying even when her hip was dislocated. On that occasion we drove several miles to the doctor who sent us to a hospital even further away. There, they took her into surgery, put her under and replaced the hip joint. At no time during all this did she fuss. Katie was and is tough.

While still on our western trip, Kathleen began acting oddly. She was thirteen years old when Pat was killed and shortly afterwards became anorexic. Her behavior, though she maintained her scholastics, was irrational despite constant counseling. Finally, we had to hospitalize her for her own good. She was diagnosed by the County Mental Health Director as bipolar. Katie became increasingly resentful as we tried to deal with her deteriorating judgement. She had always been willful and independent, a better student than her siblings and now was successful in misrepresenting her condition to others. She convinced neighbors, friends and relatives to shelter her. It never lasted long. She was always home after a short while.

Over the next several years, Katie spent time in private hospitals and in the state mental health facility a total of fourteen times. When she was 22 years of age, she signed a contract with her counselor at the state hospital agreeing to take her medication if allowed home for Christmas. Subsequently, Mariann caught Katie faking the act of taking her medicine. An argument ensued and Katie stormed off to her room in the lower walkout level. Sometime later, I checked on her for lunch and discovered she had left. It had snowed and was cold, just a few days before Christmas.

The police put out an "all-points bulletin" but missed catching Katie at various truck stops. She may have been heading to my brother Dick's home in Aspen. Days later, we received a phone call from the

Kansas City Police. They wanted her dental records to compare to the teeth in a body found in a lake. Fortunately, a few hours later, we got another call from a hospital in Denver. The police found Katie in a roadside snowbank. After she was stabilized, she was entered into a mental health program where clients receive good care, living in a house together with good supervision. They were allowed to come and go but must take their medicine every day.

Katie's present home is in Boulder, CO where she has been living for 32 years. We visited her there several times. The last time was with her sister Shannon and Shan's husband, Greg. Katie is usually friendly but not necessarily affectionate. The last time the four of us visited, we rented a house and phoned Katie. She refused to see us for three days. She was miffed because we arrived before she had wanted. At times, we are unable to make contact with Katie and we suspect that she is in the hospital as a result of not taking her meds. Neither her counselor nor the nurses at the hospital are allowed to tell us if Katie is in the hospital. They did tell us that they would contact us if it were a serious situation. Katie has her own subsidized apartment in a nice area of Boulder, a telephone, computer and her own daily schedule and friends. She seems relatively happy and safe and we are relieved.

Katie uses the name Fritzgerald. Fitz is simply a prefix in the Norman language for "son of" and Gerald is the family name. After the Normans conquered England and some Norman Fitzgeralds went to Ireland, they were called Geraldines. Katie's combining the ancestral names of Fritz and Gerald makes sense and it suggests her ancestral origins.

Mike

Michael "Mike" Fitzgerald

Before his brother Pat died, Mike was happy-go-lucky kid and a lot of fun. He was a fast sprinter and a power running back on his school football team. Mike could shalom down our steep hill flawlessly. He liked to draw and was good at it; especially with caricatures. Mike's class at St. Thomas had shared time with Lundahl public school. His art class at Lundahl was molding clay and producing ceramic figures. The instructor at Lundahl showcased Mike's figures in the school entrance hall. One figure was of a tall, thin, ascetic looking nun and the other of a squat, beefy "Broom Hilda" type nun. Both were easily recognizable by anyone that knew St. Thomas' principal and Mike's home room teacher. Broom Hilda even had the jowls and big flabby ankles of the nun. Together the nuns attended a Teachers' Conference at Lundahl and saw their images displayed. They were outraged and suspended Mike forthwith without a hearing. Of course, they had to reinstate Mike when Mariann called and assured them that it was not a malicious act. As previously stated, Mike was mischievous and liked doing caricatures.

After Pat died, Mike began smoking pot fairly often. His conduct became a concern. One day in November, he refused to rake the fallen leaves saying it was too difficult a job. I raked up the leaves in a short time, but the confrontation brought the problem to the fore. Mike was then 19 years of age and I told him to leave. "He was on his own."

Mike hitchhiked to Denver where he responded to a newspaper ad for sharing an apartment with a man working as a tile setter. When the man's girlfriend came over, Mike was too naive to allow them privacy and was told to get out for good.

Then Mike hitched to Aspen to visit my brother Dick and family. My parents were also visiting at the time. The morning after arriving, Mike drank most of the coffee before the others had any. Dad gave Mike some money and told Mike to leave. He slept in churches and park benches on the way home but made it back safely and triumphantly. His attitude had improved, and he was allowed to live with us again.

When Mike was 22 years old, he enlisted in the Navy. His decision to join the Navy was influenced by his cousin Billy, or my brother Bill's son, William III. Billy was a decorated Marine who later died from exposure to the toxic fumes he was exposed to during the Gulf War. Three years after his enlistment, while serving on the U.S. aircraft carrier Dwight D. Eisenhower at Norfolk, VA, Mike was run over by a car driven by an Air Force officer coming home from a party after midnight. It was Halloween 1985. The driver said he thought Mike was a scarecrow laying in the road on a four-lane divided highway. Mike had been on leave helping celebrate a friend's birthday. He had fallen out of the back of a pickup truck while returning to his ship.

Mike was dragged quite a way and died that night in the hospital. Two sailor buddies accompanied his body home for the military burial. At their request, I phoned their ship's captain to ask for a few day's extension of their leave. It was granted and the captain also said that Mike had done a great job cooking for the crew. The church was crowded for Mike's funeral and Mariann's cousin did a great job singing "The Minstrel Boy" during the ceremony. Mike was buried with full military honors and Mariann was presented with the flag that had draped Mike's coffin.

Mariann and I had always been proud of both Pat and Mike. Losing both of them was devastating. We tried to "drown our sorrows" with liquor for a while but neither of us has indulged now in over 30 years. A couple who lived nearby lost two of their three sons in separate car accidents a year apart. The husband wondered if there was a "curse" on our street. A few years prior, a friend had given us a Balinese wooden mask of Rangda, their god of pestilence and death. We were not terribly superstitious, but we got rid of the mask.

Shannon

Shannon was an agreeable, easygoing girl and no problem until her brother's death. She was popular with boys and girls in her school and some of the boys were particularly fond of her. She was quick witted and a good learner, more apt to be influenced by others than her sister would be.

When Shannon was finishing her junior year in high school, she ran away with a girlfriend. Shannon's friend was also an intelligent and beautiful seventeen-year-old girl. She had a friend living with friends her age in Alabama. The girls hitchhiked and were lucky. The first truck driver to give them a lift and phoned ahead for another to bring them safely to Alabama. One of the young men secretly phoned the girl's parents who immediately drove down and brought the girls home.

Shannon refused to return to the same high school for her senior year. We arranged with my brother Dick and his wife Sally to take Shannon under their care for her senior year in Aspen. After several months Shannon moved in with a wild and wealthy young woman. Shannon did not graduate but later qualified for Junior College admission in Illinois. While still in Aspen, she managed a fast food diner. One day while hitchhiking to work, she was picked up by John Denver who lived in the area. Shan wouldn't admit she knew who he was, and he did not say either. Before leaving Aspen, Shannon met some hippies from California who had converted to Jehovah's Witnesses. They converted Shannon who has been a dedicated Witness ever since.

Shannon quit school in her senior year at Aspen High but earned her GED later. After returning to Illinois, Shan attended Elgin Community College. One day, her psychology teacher talked about the case of a patient at the Elgin Mental Health Center. The patient was bipolar and did not want to take her medication. Her doctor tried an experiment, videotaping their discussions over a period of five days during which the client received no medication. After the five days, the film was shown to the doctor, the client and the client's parents together. The changes in facial expressions and behavior during the five days was dramatic. From a pretty, child-like appearance, the patient appeared gradually to look like a wild girl. Even she seemed shocked when viewing the film but claimed she hadn't been sleeping well. Shannon was able to add details for her instructor since she was Katie's sister.

All's Well

The experiment was successful but not effective. Kathleen has never acknowledged her need for medication.

Mariann, Kathleen and I drove to Aspen to pick up Shannon for our lengthy trip to California, Oregon and back to Illinois. Mike elected to stay home and work. On that trip we spent a day and a night in Yosemite National Park. The lodge was full, so we spent the night in what they called "luxury camping" facilities. These facilities were crude, cave-like structures of concrete with the open front covered by a canvas flap. We rented bedding for the steel frame bunkbeds and firewood from the lodge. We all had a good laugh about our luxury facilities. There was some concern about the nuisance of black bears, but we enjoyed the experience and slept well.

At the age of 28, Shannon finally consented to marry Greg Kildare who had been ardently courting her for almost five years. Shannon wanted the marriage ceremony to be held on our property where she had spent most of her life. Her fellow Witness friends erected a lovely flower covered arbor in our yard and we rented a large tent for dining next to the tennis court. A DJ was engaged for music and the tennis court used for a dance floor.

I removed the four by fifty-foot balcony on the back of the house as a precaution. It was eighteen years old and too many people at one time could cause it to collapse. I was also able to finish staining the cedar siding just in time before the first guests arrived. The herculean efforts of our beloved neighbors saved the day. The last

Mariann, Shannon, Greg, Bob

minute improvements may have exasperated certain family members, but it was a wonderful wedding. We all were fond of Greg. They both were radiant. When they left for their honeymoon and the guests were gone, Mariann and I were alone for the first time in thirty years.

Greg attended a junior college in a Chicago suburb while working in a factory after they were married. He then got his bachelor's degree from De Paul University in Chicago. From there he received a scholarship to William & Mary College in Williamsburg, Virginia for a master's degree in public policy. Shannon worked there as a salesclerk in the Williamsburg Foundation store where Glen Close, a William & Mary graduate, was a favorite customer of hers.

All's Well

After Greg received his degree, they moved to Santa Monica, California. Shannon preceded the movers and was able to secure a nice apartment in a rent-controlled building within walking distance of Santa Monica Beach and the Rand Corporation headquarters where Greg had a scholarship for his Doctorate Degree. Today, Greg is Chief Risk, Safety and Asset Management Officer for the Los Angeles Metro Transit Authority.

For the first several years in L.A., Shan worked selling furniture. Her impressive sales record landed her a position as the Representative of the Baker Furniture Mfg. Co. Eventually, Shannon left Baker and concentrated on her own interior design firm. She was successful and enjoyed the work and networking with clients. In recent years, she also passed the qualifying test to be an insurance adjuster but has been too busy with other pursuits to follow through.

Shannon and Greg have traveled extensively through Europe, the British Isles and Scandinavia; trading homes though a foreign travel program. Last year, they bought an historic house in Pulaski, Tennessee, a small college town just across the state line from Alabama. They are renting the house at present until Greg retires.

Shannon thinks I am now too old to drive, but she's wrong. I've driven well over a million miles and never had an accident or caused one. Of necessity, I drive every day and feel I am still better at it than most drivers I encounter. People age at different rates and I am still not senile or handicapped.

Changes

Now that Mariann and I were alone, the property maintenance requirements were becoming a liability. That fact together with the disuse of the pool and tennis court induced us to accept an offer from a woman desiring to rent the property. She was in the retirement home business and offered monthly payments of $2000 with an option to buy.

After taking possession of the property, the woman made timely payments for several months before the payments ceased. Excuses were made with promises to catch up soon, but it never happened. I went to observe their moving day. Several grown sons and daughters were helping. The matriarch was overseeing her sons move our washer and drying machines out. When I told them to put the machines back in their places, the oldest son, a lawyer who had recently passed the bar exam, tried to browbeat me into compliance. I responded with the threat to call the sheriff. They then put the appliances back into the laundry room.

The interior cedar walls had been painted an unnatural blue color and the waist high cabinet separating the dining and living rooms had been sawn in two. That was the extent of the changes. I advertised the property for sale, and it sold quickly. The buyer was a young Italian American that already owned fourteen pizza parlors. It was a contract sale with a substantial down payment and the balance due in two years. I tried to get our customer a mortgage with a local bank, but the gasoline tank would have to be removed and the ground decontaminated. The cost was quoted at $20,000 and that killed the deal. Not long after we left, the Chicago Tribune featured our property in their Home Section. The full-page article with photos stated that the new owner was only changing the roof and incorporating a cathedral ceiling. Years later, Shannon visited and spoke with the owner. He had filled in the swimming pool for parties.

It was 1989, Mariann's mother had been living with us for thirteen years, and my folks had moved from Chicago to McHenry county to be near us. My mom had been acting strangely and was diagnosed with Alzheimer's. Before moving to the suburbs, Mom had a swine flu shot against her doctor's advice. Like quite a few others that received the vaccine, she became violently ill and never fully recovered. Since she is the only one of an extended family to contract Alzheimer's, we believe it may be the result of that swine flu shot.

Our parents needed our help and we decided to find a house to live in together. In a short time, a large English country house on seven acres with a spring fed pond came to our attention. We all liked it and the price was reasonable, so we agreed to buy it. The contract purchase was with a substantial deposit and the balance due in two years. While living there, the only problem was with the owner's son and daughter-in-law. The son assumed the role of overseer of the property and would inspect the grounds without notice. His wife was Asian with an empirical attitude. One day I caught the husband, under her supervision, digging a posthole well into our lot at the edge of the driveway. They shared the paved driveway with us, and they intended to erect a gate behind our house across the driveway. I interfered and she went crazy when her husband would not defy me. They finally put the gate on their property, but I was now ready to move at the first opportunity.

My mother was difficult to care for at times, but my father made things worse. He was depressed because of Mom's condition and also because he could not make all the decisions himself. There were some lighter moments, such as the time I had to be very firm in trying to stop Mom's constant talking while in the same bedroom at night. (It was my job watching over her at night.) The next morning at breakfast Mom said, "Bob, there was a mean man in my bedroom last night."

Before a year had passed, my brother Bill sent a corporate plane to bring our parents to Ocean Springs, Mississippi, where he and

Colleen now lived. At their departure, Mom asked me where they were going and I told her, "On a vacation to see Bill and Colleen." Mom said, "Is that all?" She had doubts. The next time we saw Mom she was on life support in a hospital in Ft. Myers, Florida where Bill and Colleen had moved. Not long afterward Bill's lawyer, with the written consent of the family, got a court order to take Mom off life support. She still had a strong heart when she died at 92 years of age.

Mariann and I had visited Galena, Illinois a couple of times already when we decided to look there for a special piece of property to buy. The area, known as the Bed & Breakfast capitol of the Midwest had been the home of Ulysses S. Grant, Union Commander during the Civil War. It is located in the capitol city of Jo Daviess County and is the largest town with a population of only 3,400. Mariann said the area reminded her of Ireland even before the hotel with a pub had transplanted there from Ireland.

She wanted to have a Bed and Breakfast business in the countryside, and we found the ideal property. It consisted of 76 acres with a cold-water stream and about 50 acres of beautiful woodland. The woods connected to woodlots on the adjacent properties, making it ideal for wildlife and nature appreciation hikes.

When we satisfied the contract on the English country house, we listed the property for sale and bought the 76 acres in Jo Daviess County. Before long, we were able to sell and move to a rental house on Apple Canyon Lake close to the intended Bed and Breakfast site.

The same architect that had designed our original house on the 21 acres, was engaged for the B&B house plans.

The real estate broker that handled the purchase of the 76 acres provided a list of approved builders. The broker's brother had built a Bed and Breakfast house for friends of ours and they recommended him. The broker's list did not include her brother's name. We assumed it was for reasons other than competency. Too late, we found it was for incompetency. The brother was an alcoholic and not trustworthy. After the house was almost completed, he sued us for extra money. He lost the case, but lawyers dragged it out for four years and both of us had to pay a bundle in legal fees.

Initially, we intended to book guests for weekends only. Many guests were world travelers or otherwise very interesting people. We soon began taking guests for weekdays. Many came repeatedly over the nine years we operated. We had a great time and Brookside, as it was named, and it became quite popular. We charged appreciably less than most of the fifty or so Bed and Breakfasts in the area and it was situated in a beautiful location on a hill with two streamside ponds teeming with rainbow trout. The trout were stocked as fingerlings and fed with Purina trout pellets. They churned the water wildly when the pellets were thrown on the surface. The trout grew fast on the pellets and weighed several pounds in a couple of years.

Some of our guests wanted to learn fly casting and were willing to pay for the lessons. Eventually, the trout reached trophy

Bob age 62
Rainbow trout caught fly fishing

size—up to twelve pounds. A few avid fishermen visited just to catch a wall-hanger. Some, including our UPS deliveryman, were willing to pay surprising amounts for a big rainbow trout. In a few cases, I did not charge anything. These cases included the UPS driver, friends, family and the Dean of the Graduate School at Bradley University. The Dean stopped to ask if he and his wife could picnic on our scenic front acre. When he noted the ponds with the large trout, he said they were returning from a less than successful trout fishing trip out west. Since he was an avid and experienced fellow trout fisherman, I told him to go ahead and fish for the one he did not get on his trip. He cast from the bridge over the channel while his wife filmed the action. After he landed a nice rainbow, he gave me several special flies. We were both pleased. We also sold some of the large trout to the Number One restaurant in Galena. They paid up to $40 a fish.

The lodge accommodations were impressive with huge stone

fireplaces on both levels and all guest rooms with sliding glass doors to the outside decks. The five bedrooms and 5 1/2 baths were usually sufficient to handle all requests for a certain time. There were nature trails and tree stands for hunting and viewing wildlife in the 50-acre woods. I became a proficient archer and was able to supply venison and wild turkey for the menu.

Mariann and I had been doing all the work ourselves except for one day a week. In addition to cleaning and maintaining the premises, I cut down the dead trees, split and cured the wood and sold what we did not need. Mariann did a great job baking and serving elegant breakfasts. Guests lingered long at the breakfast table. The table faced a glass wall through which many different birds were seen at the feeders.

Mariann thought that guests would rather tell their stories than listen to mine, but I disagreed. After all, many guests returned, and I don't believe it was to finally be able to tell their stories. Actually, they all had a chance to speak—at times.

Brookside Bed & Breakfast

Ireland

In the year 2002, Mariann and I flew to Ireland with Shannon and Greg. We landed at the Shannon airport and rented a car before checking into the hotel in Limerick. The next morning, we drove to Castle Gregory on the Dingle Peninsula.

Michael Fitzgerald, my great grandfather and his son Maurice, came to America from Castle Gregory in 1846. The pastor of the church there had just left on a trip and we were unable to review the church records for our family. We stayed that night at a nearby Bed and Breakfast and ate dinner at a small inn seated around a peat fire. The burning peat had a somewhat pungent, but pleasant odor.

The following day we drove around the peninsula and secured lodging for the night at another B&B in Dingle. That evening we took in the entertainment at a local pub. The band played and sang some rousing rebel songs such as "Only the Rivers Run Free" as well as "Galway Boy" and "Danny Boy."

All's Well

From there we had planned to drive the "Ring of Kerry" road along the rugged coast but the road was closed due to heavy fog. Instead we drove directly to Killarney and from Muckross through the Killarney National Park. By mistake we got off the main road, went through an open gate over a flooded road and past a dramatic waterfall. There was a foot or more of water over the road, but it was exciting, and we made it through safely.

Our next stop after the town of Cork was Kinsale, a pretty little town on the coast. We stayed the night at another Bed and Breakfast there before moving on to Waterford. We did not kiss the Blarney Stone on the way, maybe because an Irish woman told us that young boys pee on the stone at night.

We toured the glass factory at Waterford and were fascinated watching the artisans making the glass products. The company, I understand, has gone out of business since our visit.

From Waterford we drove to the coast and ferried to the island castle that for eight centuries had been the home of Fitzgeralds. They included the Earls of Kildare, the Knights of Glin, and Mary Francis Fitzgerald. Mary Francis had dominated her social world when she was engaged to be married to Arthur Wellesley, the Duke of Windsor in 1800. The Duke later defeated Napoleon in the Battle of Waterloo and afterwards became the Prime Minister of England. Mary Francis broke off the engagement in 1801 to marry her first cousin, John Purcell.

The Duke spent the next several years in India fighting rebellious tribes. The Duke has some ancestors who were also Fitzgeralds and had under his command in India a Lieutenant Fitzgerald, brother of one of the Duke's best friends. The lieutenant was killed in battle by the sultan's troops and twelve of his men were captured. They were killed by Hindu "strong men" with nails driven into their skulls.

After years of fighting in India, the Duke returned to England to marry his betrothed, Catherine Pankenham. Her father was the commanding general that attacked New Orleans at the end of the War of 1812. He was killed by Andrew Jackson's volunteers and shipped back to England in a barrel of rum. The Duke was shocked at the sight of his faded, thirty-four-year-old bride and whispered to his clergyman brother, "She has grown ugly, by Jove."

As we entered the castle's elegant reception area, I was surprised by the large Fitzgerald crest woven into the center of the massive rug covering the floor. The crest was identical to the one we had at home. After introducing ourselves, we were ushered into the Edward Fitzgerald Room right off the reception area. Edward Fitzgerald, son of Mary Francis, is famous for his translation into English verse of Omar Khayyam's Rubaiyat. You may be familiar with some of the verses such as; "Come fill the cup and in the fires of spring, your winter garments of repentance fling, the bird of time has but a little way to fly, and lo, the bird is on the wing." Another favorite is, "I sent my soul to eternity, some letter of that aftermath to spell, and by and by my soul returned to me and said, 'You yourself are Heaven and Hell.'"

We ordered scones and coffee and Greg ordered Irish Whiskey. Our order was brought in on a beautiful tray and silver service together with a check for only $5.00! We felt quite privileged.

Eddie Kearns bought the island and castle in 1987. He opened its beauty to all visitors by developing it into a luxurious hotel and country club. If you ever go to Ireland, be sure to visit there.

Next, we drove north to Kilkenny, a good size town where we secured lodging at a B&B. Shannon arranged our nine-day trip through a friend and travel agent in Los Angeles. We had a directory to all the B&Bs in the area we were visiting. Those that charged only $65 a night were in the majority. I don't think Mariann and I spent over $2,000 including airfare for the entire trip. Of course, the year was 2002 and the Irish economy hadn't surged yet. That night Shan and Greg wanted to go to a pub that advertised entertainment. Mariann did not feel up to it but I went along. The pub was crowded, and we sat near the entrance on benches along the wall. There was a three-piece band on a small platform along the same wall and a large room beyond. The bar ran along the wall opposite the band and us. The band leader kept calling for volunteers to come and perform. There were no responders at one point and finally, Shan pulled me to my feet and said aloud, "Come on Dad, you're the only man here." It was somewhat of a surprise; she could not have had more than one beer by then.

The crowd cheered us on, and I reluctantly went to the platform with Shan. She then asked, "What should we sing?" Not wanting to sing another Irish song, I replied, Let's sing "O'Leary's Bar," a college drinking song.

I thought Shan nodded agreement, so I began singing but I was singing by myself and without accompaniment. Neither Shan nor the band knew the lyrics.

> T'was a cold winters evening
>
> The guests were all leaving
>
> O'Leary was closing the bar
>
> When he turned and he said
>
> To the lady in red
>
> Get out! You can't stay where you are
>
> She wept a sad tear in her bucket of beer
>
> As she thought of the cold night ahead
>
> When a gentleman dapper stepped out of the phone booth
>
> And these are the words that he said
>
> Her mother never told her
>
> The things a young girl should know
>
> About the ways of college men
>
> And how they come and go.
>
> Now, age has taken her beauty
>
> And sin has left its sad scar

But remember your mother and sisters, boys

And let her sleep under the bar.

Greg rushed up to compliment me and there was some applause, but I was not asked for an encore.

The next day we visited the cathedral where a Butler family member was interned. The Butlers had been rivals of the Fitzgerald's and are considered along with the Fitzgeralds as the most prominent of the "Anglos" in Ireland. There is a framed picture found throughout Ireland in gift shops showing "The Door of Reconciliation." The wooden door has a large hole in the center. In 1492, the Earl of Ormond, a Butler, fled into the Chapter House to escape from Gerald Fitzgerald, the Earl of Kildare. Fitzgerald pleaded with Butler to accept a truce. To show good faith, Fitzgerald hacked a hole in the door and thrust his arm through. It was accepted.

The Butlers sided with the English when the Fitzgeralds revolted. Eventually, King Henry VIII had all six of the leading Fitzgeralds executed. Henry then sent his henchman, Thomas Cromwell, to Ireland to find the remaining Fitzgerald heir, a boy. Irish sympathizers got the boy to France where he was protected by the French and the Pope. In later years the boy, Gerald Fitzgerald, now a young man, tried to raise an army to depose Henry but failed. Not until 1556 was Gerald able to return to Ireland as the Earl of Kildare.

From Kilkenny we drove to the Rock of Cashel near Tipperary. The Rock of Cashel was established as the official seat for the Church of Ireland in 1102. It had been largely burned down by the Earl of Kildare. After touring the ruins, I asked the young Irishman in the office why the Earl had set fire to the abbey. He replied that the Earl thought the Bishop was inside. I thought the reply was probably in typical Irish jest until reading otherwise in a book written by Winston Churchill.

Our next stop was Bunratty Castle near Limerick and the Shannon Airport. There we compared experiences with a group of young women from New York. Two of their drivers said they had lost side vision mirrors due to the narrow and congested (town) roads. Shannon also lost a mirror on our rental car. Either the girls had poor peripheral vision or were simply inexperienced. When we turned the car in, the attendant at the rental agency said we shouldn't worry about the mirror. It happened all the time and he had a barrel full of broken mirrors.

Tourists 70 years of age and older are not allowed to drive in Ireland.

Henry, our Cuban, also toured Ireland. He and his wife stopped to ask directions of a couple of bikers. Henry said they were foreigners and he could not understand what they said. Most likely they were Irish and speaking Gaelic; the native language is still spoken is some areas.

Our Irish trip was finished. It was particularly satisfying for me because of the ancestral connection but I think most people would enjoy Ireland even if not of Irish extraction. The people are friendly and they particularly like "Yanks." The land is different and quite enchanting.

Interesting Places

Mariann and I visited many state and national parks and monuments. We toured Yellowstone and Yosemite twice. These two parks should be at the top of any list of best places to visit. Following is a list of other "best places" as far as we can remember: San Antonio, Texas; Santa Fe, New Mexico; Sedona, Arizona; and Tijuana or Nogales, Mexico. These border towns may not be Mexico at its best, but they are close and interesting.

Julian, California, an old mining town about 40 miles inland from San Diego, is noted for apple pie. Apples won't grow in the lower levels there. There's also a quaint museum with unusual objects. Las Vegas, Death Valley, Reno, and Rocky Mountain National Park in Colorado, where you can drive 11,000 feet for panoramic views and see a big horned sheep herd are also wonderful. Dinosaur, Colorado has complete dinosaur skeletons. Flaming George, Wyoming National Recreational Area, Black Hills; Mt. Rushmore, South Dakota; New

England, Cape Cod; Washington, D.C.; Colonial Williamsburg, Virginia and Virginia Beach; Jamestown with huts and costumed actors in the stockade also make the list. Jefferson's Monticello, Appomattox, all near Richmond, Virginia, and the Blue Ridge Parkway—to the west leads either north toward Gettysburg or south to The Great Smoky National Park are beautiful. The Smokies were named by the Cherokee Indians and refer to the mist rising from the moist woodlands. Cades Cove in the Great Smoky National Park contains an early settler's village with rustic cabins, farm buildings and a visitor's center.

South of the park is Chattanooga and Lookout Mountain and Desoto Falls in Georgia and Alabama. Desoto State Park and Little River Canyon National Preserve feature a series of waterfalls along Little River running through rugged, rocky terrain. A short drive west in Alabama is Russell Cave, a National Monument used by Native Americans for 900 years. It has a very wide opening allowing the morning sun to reach the rear of the shallow cave. Mannequins in native dress are displayed in the cave and there is also a visitor center. Further west, Interstate 64 crosses the Natchez Trace. The Trace runs over 400 miles from Natchez, Mississippi to Nashville, Tennessee. It is a historic trail mapped by the French in the early 1700s. The lower part was Choctaw land with Natchez and Chickasaws living farther north. In the early 1800s barges loaded with goods and produce from the North delivered them via the Mississippi River to New Orleans.

They were unable to return against the strong current of the river. The barges were dismantled, and the parts sold. The riverboat men walked or rode back north by way of the Trace. The Trace is now a beautiful, isolated parkway. All commercial businesses are off the Parkway and hidden from sight behind woodlands. There is little traffic and the route is without trucks, intersections or stops. There are relics of rustic old inns and a few cabins off the Trace such as a French village where we stopped for lunch. A donkey there was walking in a circle pushing a wood shaft that activated a well pump. There are places along the Trace when you can stop and read the history of the area. Toward the northern end of the Trace there is a monument to Meriwether Lewis. He was shot and killed there at an inn in the early 1800s. It is not known whether he committed suicide or was murdered.

The Trace passes within 50 miles of Vicksburg. Vicksburg and Gettysburg were the most important battles of the Civil War. Both battles were won by the United States on the same day—the 4th of July. Coincidentally, both Tomas Jefferson and John Adams, founding fathers, died the same day—on the 4th of July.

Just outside of Nashville is the Hermitage, home of Andrew Jackson, victor over the British at New Orleans in 1815 and 7th President of the United States.

When we reached Seattle on our first trip, we took a ferry to Whidbey Island, hired a guide and fished Puget Sound. We caught a lot of salmon and cod and had a shore dinner, cooking the fish on spits over the fire. From Whidbey we ferried to the Olympic Peninsula and up Mount Olympus. Mariann and I fished both the Atlantic and Pacific Oceans several times and I fly fished the Yellowstone, the Hoh, and various Colorado trout streams.

Fortunately, we never had a really bad experience during our many travels. We did run out of gas one night outside a small desert town after driving through Death Valley. Finally, a good Samaritan stopped late at night and then brought some gas for us.

Another time, Mariann's purse was taken from the car while we were walking along the isolated Oregon ocean shore. The purse was found along the roadside and mailed to us. A thank you and reward was then sent to the finders. Only the cash was missing from the purse.

A couple of times we were lucky when faced with a serious predicament. While driving up the narrow dirt road to the summit of Mount Olympus, our new car lost traction on the loose gravel after making a sharp turn just before the summit. While holding the brake pedal down, I looked over my shoulder. There was no guardrail and it appeared to be a thousand-foot drop to the rocks below. I told Mariann to get out, but she refused. It was a very tense moment. The climb up the last twenty feet as so steep that I thought we might slide backwards if I took my foot off of the brake pedal. There was no choice, I had to ease the gas pedal down while slowly releasing the brakes. As we made it to the top, we gave thanks for the answer to our prayers.

There had been warning signs on the road below to travel at your own risk. That was not sufficient as the road up the mountain was obviously not finished. A possible explanation for the carelessness might be the lack of traffic and it being in the year 1956. On another occasion we were going to Tijuana, Mexico, just south of San Diego, where we looked for a place to park and then took a bus to Tijuana. We could not find parking or a place to get off the road. There were signs warning not to bring a gun into Mexico and I had forgotten there was a gun in the car. It was a one-way road and it was not advisable to make a U-turn. We entered Mexico with a gun! There was a parking lot and cabstand just inside the gate, so I parked and hired a cab to take us shopping. When were finished and returned to our car, I hired a young man to take us to the road leading back to the States. The Mexican customs official at the gate waved us through without inspecting our car. As Shakespeare said, "All's well that ends well."

In 2001, on the way to Florida, Mariann had a heart attack. Following treatment at a small-town clinic she was transported by ambulance, 40 miles at high speed to Tallahassee Memorial Hospital for treatment. After returning home she received a stent in her carotid artery. It was time to retire again.

Mariann and I sold the property and bought a home at Apple Canyon Lake. We enjoyed living there during the next ten years. Mariann was active in the church helping others and developed a group of close friends. I entered the horseshoe tournaments, practiced often, and won first place several times. There was a beautiful nine-hole golf course in the development where I had membership. I regret having never taken a lesson, but I did as well as most of the members.

During the winter months, Mariann and I vacationed either to South Padre Island, Texas or Green Valley, Arizona near Nogales, Mexico. Several couples from Apple Canyon Lake vacationed with us at South Padre Island. We shopped the Mexican border towns and Mariann had dental work done in Progresso, Mexico. The dentist did a good job. He studied at the University in Mexico City and had been a dentist in Crystal Lake, Illinois. There were many offices in Progresso and prices were about a third of those in the States.

In Arizona, I tramped the desert and mountains almost daily looking for artifacts, meteorites and anything of interest. I wore a sidearm for self-defense. Once a border patrol agent stopped his jeep to talk. He may have been checking to see if I was an illegal. He offered to give me a lift to my car, but I declined. I had a GPS, but it was not necessary as there are mountain ranges both to the east and west for guide points. Another time, Mariann and I were driving a long way through uninhabited desert to visit a small ghost town. The dirt road eventually deteriorated with water streaming across. I was able to turn around and start heading back when we saw several men with large backpacks sneaking through the vegetation. Mariann yelled not to stop which I was not considering anyway. After several miles we came to a temporary border patrol check point. I told the agents what we had seen. They believed the men were carrying sacks of marijuana and they radioed for a helicopter to look for them.

I had seen many places in my desert wanderings where refugees had rested, left empty containers and in some cases had been met by confederates bringing food and clothing. Dirty clothing and even tennis shoes were discarded.

Plymouth, Massachusetts Replica of the Mayflower

Jamestown, Virginia

Austria & Germany

In 2006, Mariann and I, with Shannon and Greg, flew to Munich, Germany during the Oktoberfest. We were invited to stay at the home of a woman friend of Shannon. Diethilda, also a Witness, spent winters in Los Angeles with her two sons and grandchildren. Diethilda proved to be a good guide for Munich and spoke some English.

The festival's entertainment area reminded me of a large carnival with booths for games of chance, food and drink purveyors, and a variety of rides, including a giant Ferris wheel that Mariann and Shan tried. They were thrilled. There were seven huge beer halls, all filled up most of the time. When we were able to enter one, we were seated at a large picnic type table. At the table were two German male college students with who we conversed in a friendly but limited way. Few of the people we met in Germany and Austria spoke English well.

After having two very large steins of beer each, in about thirty minutes time, we were asked to leave. According to Diethilda, the waiter said we weren't drinking fast enough. Mariann and I drank only nonalcoholic beer and already had as much as we could handle so leaving was not a problem. Mariann said that some of the older women were also rude and had pushed her out of their way while walking in a crowd there.

The next morning, we said, *"Auf wiedersehen and dankeschon,"* to Diethilda and left. Shannon drove the rental car as always. On the trip we stayed mostly at B&Bs called pensions, and we used a guidebook to find the most interesting places.

Most of the following is taken from Mariann's notes: We stopped at Nymphenburg Palace, a lovely Italianate style palace, overwhelmingly rococo with beautiful grounds and separate hunting lodge. The latter being pink and white on tile outside and blue, white and silver inside instead of the gilt lavished on the main buildings. Greg said the Bavarian Princes still have residences in separate wings of the main palace.

From Nymphenburg on the way to Oberammergau, site of the famous Passion Play, we stopped for lunch at the oldest working Monastery in Bavaria. It is also known for its beer, wine and authentic meals.

In Oberammergau we lodged at Sofie's Pension, the oldest building in Oberammergau. The bells tolled all night, interfering with our sleep. We started the following day with a sumptuous breakfast of fried eggs, bacon, fruit, cheeses, cold meats, good brats and coffee served in the most rosemaling room I've ever seen.

There was a small cemetery opposite the inn where many of the grave markers bore the Iron Cross indicating a military burial. Then on to Schloss Linderhof Castle about 15 minutes from Oberammergau where Leopold spend most of his last eight years.

Leopold's next castle, Neuschwanstein, is much more impressive. The awesome beauty of the palace, high on a mountain, overlooking a deep gorge has been often shown in children's book and Disney productions, Ludwig's "Over the Top" extravaganza is his last. His hobby seemed to be building opulent castles. He lived like some fairy price—some might say "Wacky Fairy."

Ludwig was very creative; he even had an elevator that brought meals to his private room. Creativity might have led to Ludwig's downfall. He kept building castles until Bavaria was almost bankrupt. He had been at Neuschwanstein only a short time when he and his doctor were both found drowned in the castle pond. Ludwig had been a good swimmer and no water was found in his lungs.

We had pictures taken on a foot bridge spanning the gorge before leaving for Riette. Along the way we stopped at a Fortress Museum that may have been Roman, then Austrian. It was very romantic. Continuing on, we found a nice pension on the outskirts of Riette. That evening we had a fabulous dinner way up in a small chalet in the middle of nowhere. It had been recommended by a lady at the

Fortress Museum.

Greg woke us up at 7:20 in the morning. Our pension was located in a picturesque valley. The innkeepers were twin brothers and they had a huge dog, a combination of Wolfhound and St. Bernard. The dog silently ogled us we ate breakfast. Klaus called ahead for us to my cousin, Alois Hann, to expect us at Ladis. The drive from there to Ladis was breathtaking. There were glorious vistas in every direction.

Alois' wife Deanna fixed a lovely lunch which we shared with the family including two young girls and the older boy of twelve. Alois then brought us to his mother's place in the original Hann house. It was a very large, three story stone building. Their Hann ancestors had been knighted by the Holy Roman Emperor Frederick III.

Alois' mother was very warm and gracious with us. After the visit with her we went to the close by bar owned by Alois' sister, Roswitha, and her husband, Harold. We spent about an hour there buying rounds for all.

Alois insisted that we stay the night in one of the apartments he owned. His side business was plumbing, and he had a job scheduled in nearby Italy (15 miles away) early in the morning. That morning we had a German breakfast of cheese, cold cuts, fruit and rolls. Deanna had kept her son Andreas home from school, we suspect, to act as interpreter although he was not a lot of help at interpreting.

Because Alois' main business was lodging, we left 80 Euros in our room and said our goodbyes. We were disappointed that we did not get to meet the other brother, Alex, who was in Innsbruck at a convention. Alex owned a ski shop in Ladis.

Our next stop was Ischgl where my grandfather, Anton Fritz was born. The house he had lived in was now owned by a doctor and no one was at home. The mountains, villages, rushing streams with waterfalls, interspersed with church steeples and an occasional fort or tower along the way were picture perfect.

We stopped at the museum in Ischgl where the curator told us that there were several Fritz shops in town. As far as I have been able to ascertain, however, my great grandmother, Theresa, was the only child surviving the Joseph Fritz family other than my grandfather Anton. Records from Austrian archives list Anton as the illegitimate son of Franz Joseph the emperor. Joseph Fritz was the emperor's representative in Ischgl. My great grandmother, Theresa, was given a farm and pension by Franz Joseph to be passed to her son Anton.

From Ischgl we drove to Innsbruck and were lucky to find rooms at Margaret's pension on the outskirts as Innsbruck was hosting a big convention. The following day we visited the Hapsburg summer home palace in Innsbruck and the Fold Museum.

Mariann writes: What a lovely old town on the Inn River, cobblestones and brick streets, painted buildings (some from the 12th century) balconies, gay windows and paintings on the fronts. Lots of high-end shops tucked into the narrow streets. People watching was fascinating. Greg and I did that for an hour while Bob and Shan went to the record bureau to check on Fritz records. We also visited the church built by Maximillian for his very elaborate sarcophagus. However, he was so unpopular the people wouldn't allow him to be buried there.

Leaving Innsbruck, we drove quite a distance past Strasbourg to St. Wolfgang, a charming little town on the beautiful lake Wolfgangsee, with mountains in the background. We found a lovely hotel named Margaretha with balconies overlooking the lake. There were fishing poles and bikes for our use.

Shan did a good job negotiating our extended stay. The manager was a thirty-something year old "Teutonic Hunk." His father was a diplomat assigned to Washington, D.C. My mother, when very young, had also vacationed with her family at this same lake.

Dinner that evening was in Strasburg. Greg had excellent hasenpfeffer, Bob had potato pancakes on wonderful leak sauce, I had pork steak topped with onions and fresh horseradish. Shan had German style frittata. After breakfast in the cozy hotel dining room the next morning, Bob and the kids went exploring. The adventurers did not return for five hours. They had taken a rail car up a high mountain above the tree line and walked back down on a perilous path. The kids had sore legs for a few days, but not Bob. He must have inherited Tyrolean legs from his mother.

Dinner that night was at a Mill House located up the side of a mountain by a rushing stream. The host was a typical congenial

Austrian. Bob had blue trout—I think it is brined and steamed. I had fried trout and we split, half and half. We had Bibb lettuce, sheep's cheese, hors d'oeuvres and boiled potatoes with brown bread. It was not cheap, but it was worth it. Shan and I walked around St. Wolfgang and I checked out the shops. This has to be the best time of year to visit. The hills are bursting with autumnal colors and the temperatures are just right. We decided to spend another day here at the Margaretha as home base. We spent the afternoon in Salzburg, the ancient fortress town. It is amazing how these old towns have been preserved intact through these many years. Though we spent most of the day in the Castle Fortress we did see Mozart's, St. Peter's Cathedral, and enjoyed a pastry and coffee after a sausage and kraut lunch. I have never seen such pastries!

We left Hotel Margaretha and our "Teutonic Hunk," Clemens Vogel, with a heavy heart. It was an idyllic setting with Old World ambiance and a charming, talented manager. He left for Munich to perform all weekend at Orchestra Hall as a pianist with his own group. He sold us a CD disk of pictures of St. Wolfgang and I bought a CD of his music. He gave me a great deal—I love JAZZ! And it is GREAT! It will be my prize from the trip.

From St. Wolfgang, we proceeded to the old medieval town of Melk on the Danube River where we enjoyed a late lunch at the outdoor cafe and people watched; like being in a Hollywood movie set. Pope Pious VI spent "Holy Week" in Melk in 1782 and Napoleon visited Melk twice. Haydn composed a violin concerto entitled "Melker Konzert." Melk is a very small, quaint town with all shops and restaurants on one main block.

The Benedictine Abbey is Melk's jewel. It is the center of culture and has a secondary school with 700 boys and girls being taught by monks. Monks have been living and working in the Abby for over 900 years. We spent a few hours at the beautiful baroque Abbey admiring the extensive library and artifacts it contains. What a layout! It is incredible how well it has been preserved. Mozart played the organ there when he was eleven years old.

The kids surprised us with reservations at a real castle for tonight, complete with moat, draw bridge, its own chapel, tavern and courtyard. Also, frescoes sprinkled liberally around the many rooms including our apartment. The castle is on a high hill overlooking the Danube. Even the breakfast was a treat.

Spent the next day in (Wien) Vienna and most of the time in the Hapsburg treasury. The self-guided tour was most interesting. Then lunch at a chain of deli buffets where we had our main meal. After walking our legs off, we headed back to Melk where we had booked rooms for three days. We had nice quarters with reasonable rates.

Shan, Greg and I will return to Wien tomorrow, Sunday, for more museums, the Winter Palace and the opera, the "Flying Dutchman." Bob will have to fend for himself since he doesn't enjoy any of the above.

The next day at the opera we waited an hour to get in and spent another long time up and down on different levels looking and finally squeezed into the standing room only. It was so hot and so close, I thought I'd faint. The staging and voices were terrific, but a seat is definitely required for me. Don't think my feet will ever recover. After breakfast at Gam the next day, the three of us headed back to Vienna. Bob stayed in Melk to explore an old castle/fortress and cemetery. We headed to Hapsburg Winter Palace and spent four and a half hours gazing at the many rooms and works of art. It is almost too much for one day. We ate in a Persian restaurant, a welcome change from wurst, pork and cabbage. We enjoyed shish kebab, hummus and great coffee.

Bob: The following day, the four of us headed back to Vienna to tour The Summer Palace—another extravaganza.

It seems incredible that the rulers got away with such lavish multiple palaces.

The afternoon was spent finding and filming Napoleonic Battlefields—Greg's hobby. Unable to locate the site of an important battle after driving around the designated area several times, we stopped for a late lunch at a corner restaurant/bar. No one there understood English so with my limited German and the help of my dictionary, I asked for the location of the battlefield. Nobody knew but later the waitress came to me to say someone that just came in knew the location. It was just around the corner; we had passed it at least twice. There were no signs at the street indicating that the two-story brick building was a museum. Apparently, it was of little interest to the locals.

The next morning, we packed our belongings and left Melk headed for Salzburg and west to the Eagle's Nest, Hider's Hideaway. It was his birthday present and over a mile high on the mountain. What a drive! A hair-raising switchback road with precipitous curves overlooking long drops to the valley below. When we reached the summit, we had to climb further on foot with spectacular views all around.

After we saw enough, we headed to Munich to hole up near the airport. We could not find anything but found a place about twenty minutes away to stay. It was nice and it was reasonable because we took attic rooms. We went to a nearby Bavarian restaurant. Like several other restaurants, there was a Capercaillie mounted on wall. The Capercaillie is a grand looking grouse-like bird that inhabits the pine forests in that part of the world. Males can weight up to twelve pounds.

Mariann writes: It has been a dream trip for me. The kids deserve medals for planning, navigating and driving on some streets that were scarcely wider than the car and paved with bricks. We are truly blessed.

Retirement

In 2011 Mariann and I drove to northeast Alabama to investigate the idea of moving there. My sister Mary and her family live in or near Huntsville, the "Rocket City." We found an older house that we liked. It is a ranch style without stairs and a large fenced yard. It is in the same section as the house where Mary and Tom live. We bought the house and moved in January 2012. I had a small pond excavated and fed by a shallow well. I built a 4 ft x 50 ft stone wall into the far bank and added a waterfall in view through the kitchen picture window. I am 90 years old now and this may be my last "Hurrah."

Back to brother Dick for a quick look at his current situation. Dick, 85 years of age at this writing, with his wife Sally have been spending the cold months in Colima, Mexico for the past 35 years. They both have dual citizenship, American and Mexican. Dick, with both hips and knees replaced has trouble with the Colorado cold season.

In Mexico, Dick and Sally own a large condo for guests and an earthquake resistant house for their own use about 15 miles north of Manzanillo on the ocean. Their oldest son was an all-state Colorado hockey player and his son, now at Notre Dame, an all-state Colorado football player and Lacrosse player. They also have another son and a daughter, both happily married.

Mary, my sister, and her husband here in Alabama, are doing well. Both look and act younger than their age. In their family the girls are athletes. All three girls had offers to college for volleyball. The 3 boys, age 45 to 62, are all doing well.

Tom and Mary Duerr

My Father

My father, William Fitzgerald, was a unique character and he had quite an interesting business career. Dad worked diligently on the family farm at all phases of crop and stock raising. He was captain of his high school basketball team; there probably was not much competition in that tiny school but Dad proved he was an athlete years later when he challenged my brother Bill and I to a race. Both Bill and I had broken or tied our high school dash records, but we narrowly beat our dad.

When Dad graduated from high school, he enrolled in a Business Administration Course at Notre Dame University in South Bend, Indiana. It was during the Knute Rockne era and Elmer Layden of the famed four horsemen was a classmate of Dad's. Dad left to join General Electric Corp. after only a year, but he did receive an honorary degree from Notre Dame years later.

Dad left General Electric before long to start a career in sales. While bringing cars from Indiana to sell in Chicago, Dad met and married my mother, a nurse at St. Elizabeth Hospital in Chicago. Mom quit nursing to raise her four children starting with William in 1926, myself, Robert in 1928, Mary in 1931, and Richard in 1933. Mom and Dad remained happily married for almost seventy years.

For twelve years, Dad sold encyclopedias "house to house." He was able to provide well for us during the Great Depression. During the Century of Progress Exposition in Chicago from 1933 to 1934, Dad received a contract from the publishers of the "Book of Knowledge," the "World Book," and the publisher of "America." He represented all three during the Exposition.

While the country was preparing for war in 1940, Dad assembled a staff of aeronautical specialists to teach aircraft mechanics and maintenance to qualified candidates who were exempt from military draft while training aircraft for study were brought to the school right through the busiest part of downtown Chicago.

When the war ended, Dad sold the school and was then asked by a woman to help rescue her failing school for teaching young women modeling. The school located on Chicago's prestigious Michigan Avenue had few students. Dad initiated an advertising and promotion program and personally dealt with all prospective clients. In a short time, enrollment swelled and when the owner reneged on the amount of commissions owed Dad, he opened his own modeling school, also on Michigan Avenue. Dad named his new school Boulevard Models. It was a big success in a short time, but before long

Dad sold the business to a wealthy man from southern Illinois. I imagine that Dad got a good price for it due to the glamour associated with the business.

Dad's next business venture was encouraged by the introduction of postage vending machines. These vending machines were being placed by private individuals in stores for the convenience of customers. Dad made arrangements for a specialized manufacturer to produce a machine that could handle postage stamp rolls. After a period of experimentation, a reliable working machine was developed, and Dad organized a salesforce for its sale to stores and other logical outlets. After graduating from the University of Illinois, I began selling the machines in Texas. The machines were priced at $79, a substantial sum in 1955, but I sold a lot of them. They proved to be an asset for almost everyone that had one.

In 1956, I married Mariann Stilwell and after a long road trip across the country together from Seattle to Miami Florida, sightseeing and selling many more stamp vendors, I quit the road and joined Dad in the offices of Fitzgerald Associates. At that time ballpoint pens were a novelty. Papermate had introduced ballpoints but they were expensive. Dad found a company in New York that was capable of manufacturing a simple, inexpensive, ballpoint pen. Machines were produced capable of vending the pens when contained in cardboard tubes. We were then able to set up distributors in various cities and we helped them get started by securing stores, schools and other logical outlets to place the vendors.

For a while, pen sales volume through the machines exceeded expectations. Too soon however, many stores began selling cheap ballpoint pens and companies began using the pens as promotional gifts. As sales volume through the machines lessened, it became apparent that further efforts to appoint distributors should be discontinued. Accordingly, distributors were authorized to reorder pens direct from the manufacturer and Dad once again began looking for a new business venture.

Before long, Dad received an offer to secure distributors for a new product produced by a large manufacturing company. The product, called Regiscope, was a dual lens camera designed to produce a picture of the person cashing a check and the check being cashed. It was used to identify the person with the check if the check bounced.

The first distributor appointed was contacted through a mailing to a select list. Following telephone conversations with Dad, the gentleman from Colorado came to the office with a cashier's check for $125,000 which was a huge amount at the time. Dad signed up a number of distributors for Regiscope during the ensuing months but then, for reasons unknown to me, withdrew from the deal with an agreement from the manufacturer that Dad would receive the commissions on reorders previously agreed to by the distributors Dad had signed.

Within the first year, distributors brought a class action lawsuit against the manufacturer for failure to correct problems with the cameras. Subsequently, the manufacturer refused to pay or settle for commissions on reorders due Dad. Fitzgerald Associates sued and won a substantial monetary award from the court against the manufacturer.

We then began experimenting with over the counter health aids. Field tests indicated that packets of four different products had favorable acceptance. They were a proven formula for the treatment of colds with four tablets at 25 cents, a concentrated vitamin for hangovers with two tablets at 25 cents, a calmative tablet with two tablets at 25 cents, and six aspirin tablets at 10 cents. These four different products were heat sealed in aperture packs, displayed on counter racks and called "Pac Aids."

As soon as we began to set up Pac Aid distributors, we received a letter from the Federal Drug Commission challenging the product descriptions printed on the packets. We had taken care to use standard and conservative descriptions, so we sought the counsel of a reputable law firm specializing in drug related issues. We were advised that some major drug manufacture were probably responsible for initiating the complaint and they would probably continue to make it difficult for us. The lawyers did not offer much hope, so after due consideration, we reluctantly decided to cut our losses and discontinue the program. Fortunately, the two distributors just appointed also decided not to take legal action.

Following that disappointment, Dad and I flew to Detroit,

Michigan to meet with a group and discuss a possible business connection. The meeting ended late and Dad and I missed our return flight on Southwest Airlines. We caught the next flight encountering rough weather and we were held up for several minutes over O'Hare International Airport. After landing safely, we learned that the flight we missed had gone down in Lake Michigan and there were no survivors. It was quite sobering.

With no business prospects in the offing, we decided to disband Fitzgerald Associates Corp. Dad accepted an offer to become Senior Editor from the publisher of the National Cyclopedia of American Biography located in New York. As the senior editor, Dad traveled nationally collecting data from family members on the lives of prominent Americans.

Dad and I were still partners, and I made a favorable connection with a versatile manufacturing company run by three Italian brothers. An agreement was made for them to produce an innovative postage vendor of my desire. They provided $25,000 cash for a prototype and permanent tools and dies to make the machines; Dad and I provided the machine design and a sales force to sell the machines. We named the new company Selectra Inc. For a few months, I worked the tool and die department perfecting a working model. The machines would be capable of dispensing from one to five stamps from one roll and if desired, one to five stamps from a second tool of the same or different denomination. This flexibility enabled the machine to handle postal rate changes. Standard coin changers allowed for the use of various type coins.

Dad made preliminary contacts with banks, chain stores and salespeople during his travels. As always, Dad was a super salesman and when the vendors were ready, he sold numerous Selectra equipment, mostly by cold calling (no inquiry) and always with check in full with each order.

Selectra stamp vendors quickly became leaders in the field and the United States Post Office became interested in the machines. After thorough testing, they approved the Selectra machines for purchase. I presented the first special Selectra postage vendor to the Deputy Postmaster at a ceremony held in the Rotunda of the United States Capitol Building.

The publicity and prestige from the association helped us sell many units to Sears, Wards, Walgreens and many supermarket chains. Eventually more than 30,000 Selectra units were sold. I received U.S. Patents on the Selectra design and on a multiproduct vendor together with a unique display rack. Dad lived happily until the age of 94. He had motivated all three of his sons to succeed in sales but none of us equaled Dad's guts, charm and expertise.

Anecdotes

Archie Lieberman, the noted photojournalist, was a friend and neighbor of ours when we were operating our Bed and Breakfast business. Archie and his wife Esther lived on an eighteen-acre farm about 34 mile from us. They had a golden retriever named Junior and two horses. Neither Archie nor Esther rode the horses, but Archie wanted to fit in with the country folk. Archie had been a marine combat photographer in the Pacific during World War II. He has since authored twenty-two books filled with his photos and their stories. "Neighbors" and "Farm Boy" are two of the most popular books. Archie's one-man shows have been on exhibit all over the United States and as far away as the Soviet Union.

Archie and I were close, and we spoke frankly to each other. Once he told me had lived with the Bedouins for two weeks and I asked if the Bedouins knew he was Jewish. At that, Archie exploded and shouted, "I am not Jewish, I am an American; I fought for this country." Another time, Archie asked who I thought the Democrats might nominate for the presidency. When I replied that Lieberman would be a good choice, Archie said that would never happen because Lieberman was Jewish. I reminded him that people said that Kennedy could not win because he was Catholic. Archie said that was different because the Kennedys had money. I replied that Jews also had money and Archie exploded again. The mention of Jews having money obviously touched a sore spot with Archie. The next morning Esther told Mariann that Archie did not think I was anti-Semitic, just anti-semantic. Every race, religion and nationality has been the object of prejudice and no one is without fault. It is puzzling, however, why Jews are among those at the forefront of the victims. As a people, Jews have demonstrated a significant degree of intelligence and their contributions to humanity have been impressive. Before he died at the age of eighty-three, Archie gave me a signed portrait he did of John Fitzgerald Kennedy, taken when Kennedy was campaigning for the presidency. Esther still calls to talk with Mariann and last year sent us a beautiful 12x15 photo of the rolling fields and homestead once owned by the subject of "Farm Boy."

***

One winter I took the family to Telemark, a ski resort in northern Wisconsin. We had learned the skiing basics on a beginners' slope near our home in Illinois. A good friend and his wife and their three kids came with us. They also had lost their oldest son when a teenager. Like us, they also had their two daughters and remaining son along for the fun. The resort hotel where we stayed had a sauna located off the hallway leading to our rooms. As we were passing by, we could see through the sauna glass wall, our daughter Katie sitting on the bench in there completely nude. She was the only occupant and hopefully thought that people could not see through the glass from the other side.

More embarrassing for me was the ski lift incident. From the time I arrived at the area, I stood out as the old guy wearing bulky clothing and a funny knit cap. My first venture on the beginners' slope was using the rope tow. Halfway up I slipped and fell causing a big pileup of kids behind me. After that, I was watched more closely. Next, Shannon coaxed me into going with her up a higher hill on the chairlift. Near the top of the hill, Shan suddenly shouted "jump" as she jumped off the chair. It was too late. I had expected to be let off after a stop at a platform. Instead, riders had to jump off the moving lift onto a small level spot about six feet square under the lift. When I reached the top of the lift at the turnaround, my presence in the chair tripped the off switch shutting down the whole system. It took a few minutes for the attendant to arrive. He ignored my request to use his ladder to help me get out of the chair. With the lift going again, I overheard several remarks concerning me as the culprit as I passed the skiers that had been stranded in their suspended chairs the entire time. Upon reaching the bottom, I immediately fled the area.

***

All's Well

Pat and Mike had taped a conversation they had together just before Pat was killed. Mariann took the tape to the TV station in Chicago where Phil Carlson, my cousin's husband worked thinking Phil might be able to improve the clarity. Phil was a renowned cameraman and a brilliant tech person. During a college All-Star game in Soldiers Field at night, all the lights went out. After a long wait, the lights came back on and Jack Brickhouse announced that Phil Carlson had fixed the problem. While Mariann was at the elevator to go up to Phil's office, Oprah Winfrey approached with her entourage and asked if she could help. Oprah then sent someone to get Phil. When he could not be found, Oprah sent another to check Phil's hangouts. When that effort failed, Oprah told Mariann that she would take the tape and see to it that Phil got it. That attitude helps explain why Oprah is so popular.

***

While driving though Nebraska on the interstate with Mariann we were suddenly engulfed by a blinding dust storm. The dust was so thick I could not see anything ahead, behind or to the side. It was a frightening situation and I was not sure what I should do. If I slowed down, I might be rear-ended and if I did not slow down, I could hit something in front of us. I tried to ease the car over to the side of the road before a collision occurred but for a while I could not see where the shoulder was located. Then I got a dim view of cars that had left the road and were at the bottom of a sharp drop off. I was able to ride the shoulder until soon we were on an exit ramp and able to see the road ahead.

***

You have to be an optimist to travel without sufficient funds, checkbook or credit card when driving an old vehicle. While driving from Chicago to the University of Illinois downstate, the old car needed a minor fix. The charge was more than I could pay. The monthly government check, $110 for vets attending classes, was waiting in Champaign. I left my shotgun to hold until I paid the amount due. It was better that it happened when it did, rather than when a beautiful young lady was along for the ride. Her name was Millie Fogel and she was a girlfriend of my brother, the Beau Brummel elect at the U of I. Millie later became famous as Barbara Baines, the blond starlet of the TV serial "Mission Impossible." She married her costar, Martin Landau. I think she was more attractive as the dark-haired Millie Fogel. I believe both Millie and Martin are gone now.

***

Almost a year after finishing my studies, I was returning to Chicago for my sister Mary's wedding. While driving through Arkansas at night, the generator in my "like new" car began to fail. When the headlights dimmed, I would turn them off temporarily until I had trouble seeing the road. I was close to a town, so I continued on. In those days, gas stations often were also auto repair shops. I was lucky finding such a station right off the highway in the well-lighted town. The only one there was a tall black man. Today, "politically correct" people use the term "African American." However, I asked a number of guests at our Bed and Breakfast who were black which term they preferred. They all said they prefer "Black" not "African American." The black mechanic replaced the generator, probably with a rebuilt. Again, I was unable to pay, although a large sum in commissions was waiting at the office. I offered as payment a used vending machine I had taken in trade. I explained that it would be worth more than the amount owed to the right person. My rescuer agreed to the trade— "Bless his heart."

Another time that I "lucked out" was when Mariann and I were coming from Death Valley to a small town near Lake Isabella, south of the Sequoia National Forest. The only lodging place off the bypass was a small motel with the "No Vacancy" sign lit. When we passed the motel there was only dark, desert like emptiness. We took the next exit to return to the little town. The engine quit as we coasted down the exit ramp to the country road below. We hadn't passed any gas stations in the high desert after leaving the Visitors Center in Death Valley or we would have stopped for gas. We had driven several hundred miles and used up more gas per mile at the higher elevations. I stood on the road by the car hoping for someone to stop. Just a single car passed before a car stopped. There were three young men in the car. Mariann thought they looked scary but as it turned out, they were good guys. The driver said he would go to get gas. When he returned with the gas, I had to insist he take payment for it. Then he led us back to the gas station where he returned the gas can and told us about a lodge at the lake where we could get a good meal and lodging for the night. We expressed our heartfelt thanks before parting. Once again, luck was with me; or was it Mariann's Guardian Angel?

We had a great dinner at the lake with fresh caught trout as the main dish. The little lake was fed by the Kern River that flows down the mountain from Sequoia National Park. I would have fished for trout the next morning but this time we had flown to Vegas and rented a car there. My fly-fishing equipment was left at home.

***

Mariann and I have been to Las Vegas a few times. We usually stayed at the Circus-Circus Hotel and Casino. We don't gamble but the rooms were very nice and the rates more than reasonable. The food was also good but the biggest attraction for us in Vegas was the shows. I particularly liked the show depicting Medieval times with jousting knights on horses. Best of all was the daily enactment of the battle between a British man-o-war and a pirate ship. The outdoor show was free of charge for everyone and viewing stands were set up in front of the small sequestered bay where the pirate ship lay anchored. The action began to dramatic music as a British ship comes around the high cliff into the bay and the battle begins. During the realistic fight, both ships sustain damage by cannon fire. Suddenly, a cannonball hits the powder magazine on the pirate ship. It explodes and the ship slowly sinks beneath the water's surface. It is an amazing sight and a mystery how it is done over and over every day.

From Lake Isabella we drove to Santa Monica to visit Shannon and Greg. They had a lovely little apartment within walking distance of the beach, Santa Monica Pier and the Promenade. Next, we went to Tijuana to shop. Tijuana was the junkiest border town that I visited. Americans go there mostly to buy pharmaceuticals.

After Tijuana, we spent several days with our good friend, Don, a Viatorial priest that had been the chaplain for our Christian Family group in Illinois. Don had permission from his superior to leave St. Viator High School where he taught to go on his own mission out west. Don initially served as the Newman Foundation Chaplain at Napa Sonoma College in California. At the time of our visit, he was a pastor of the little Catholic church in Santa Ysabel, CA, close to the Mexican border. Parishioners were composed of ranchers, Mexicans and Native Americans still called "Indians" by some people. Don had the greatest respect for the Mexicans who were hard working, family oriented; the opposite of the "Indian" men who were often drunks. He said the ranchers contributed the least but were the most demanding.

Don had been raised on a farm in South Dakota. He could be plain spoken and was later fired by his bishop for that reason. Some of the ranchers' wives had complained. Don then became a prison chaplain and parish priest for retired nuns in Tucson. He died in 2016 at the Viatorial retirement home in Illinois. He was a good man and we miss him.

From Santa Ysabel we drove up the mountain to Julian in the Cleveland National Forest. Julian was formerly a mining town and late known for its apple pies. Lowlanders from the San Diego area drove up to Julian in winter to pack snow into their pick-ups to spread under their apple trees at home. Like tulips, apple trees need some cold in winter to bloom later. There is an interesting little museum in Julian with mining equipment not usually seen elsewhere.

***

On one trip west, we visited my brother Dick's family at Lake Havasu City, AZ. The lake is an enlargement of the Colorado River and big enough for the large number of power boats owned by the residents. An original London Bridge had been dismantled in London, England and then erected at Lake Havasu. Sometime after our visit, my brother's home was looted and "desecrated" while the family was away. The culprit was later caught but unfortunately justice was not served due to the father's influence.

When Shannon was eighteen years old and still living in Aspen, Mariann, Katie and I drove to pick her up to join us on our western trip. While driving through Aspen we were stopped at a police roadblock. Cars were being searched for an escaped murder suspect. Later we learned that Ted Bundy, the notorious serial killer, had just escaped through the second story window at the rear of the local library. Bundy had been in the Aspen jail awaiting trial for the murder of a young female in nearby Snowmass, CO. He had been allowed to use the local library to "study" for defending himself in court.

During his escape, Bundy was able to find his way through woods and mountain terrain all the way to Colorado Springs where he was caught and jailed. The clever killer also managed to escape from jail there by crawling through a transom. It was a long time and many murders later before Bundy was brought to justice.

Bob's brother Dick and family

***

One afternoon while living in northern Illinois, we had a huge snowstorm. I made it home safely from the office but there was no room left in the garage to park the car. I had to leave it in the driveway in front of the house. The next morning, we had about twenty inches of snow accumulation and the temperature was dropping. I had a heater on the tractor, and it started right away. When it had warmed the hydraulic fluid sufficiently, I began clearing our 200-foot-long driveway through the woods. The snow was too deep to use the blade moving forward; it was necessary to back into the snow while raising the blade at the edge of the driveway. When our drive was finished, I dug out some of the neighbors' driveways. Theirs were much shorter and I was able to clear several in less than an hour.

By late afternoon the wind had picked up and the temperature was dropping fast. That night the weatherman announced the windchill factor was 80 degrees below zero. The next morning, I was unable to start the car. It was not until a few days later by using a heat lamp on the engine block, blankets covering the hood and less frigid temperatures that the car finally started.

Now that I am living in Alabama, I am no longer concerned about snow and ice or even cold temperatures. There are positives and negatives wherever you live.

Having spent most of the winters in northern states and driven over a million miles covering all the lower 48 states, I can offer some advice on driving. My experience driving on ice taught me that the most important thing is—Don't Do It. When driving on ice you're relying on luck. Skill may help but it is not enough.

When starting to slide, don't touch the brake or gas pedals. If a car is coming, try to steer off the road. Driving on the shoulder is better than being on the road. Driving into a snowbank, if there is one, will help prevent a collision.

Wet roads are also dangerous. Curves should be taken slowly. One summer when I was returning with the family from a farm visit, my cousin and her family were in their car following us. We were on a blacktop road and rain mixed with the oil from farm machinery had caused the road to be slippery. My cousin's husband Phil, a popular tv camera man, was driving as his car slid off the road on a curve and bounced through the shallow ditch. Their four little kids were all thrown out the back of the station wagon taking the rear window with them. For some reason, our four kids about the same ages as theirs remained in the car. I witnessed it happening all through the rear-view mirror concerned that Phil was coming too fast around the curve. It was a traumatic scene with the four little kids laying in the ditch. Fortunately, no one was seriously injured. Phil learned the hard way to drive more slowly on wet curves.

Driver education apparently is not comprehensive enough in many cases, as there are too many bad drivers. In some places it seems like there is no testing of a drivers' performance. Especially obvious are the many drivers that block the left lane. Many years ago, there were numerous signs off roadways all over the country stating, "Keep to the Right—Except when Passing."

I believe that "road rage" happens mostly when drivers block the way, holding back impatient drivers or any drivers that are in a hurry.

***

Somehow our mail carrier got one of pamphlets "Things Everyone Should Know." He asked what church we attended and seemed disappointed when I told him we were Catholic. My guess is that the few religious or philosophical segments in the pamphlet caused him to think we were Baptists like him. A short time later, he left a printed invitation in our mailbox to a Veterans Day celebration at his church.

Mariann and I attended and had a great time singing many patriotic songs along with the others. There were patriotic films shown and a short talk that included a remark that guests should not contribute to the collection. I contributed anyway to show my appreciation. Our host, the mail carrier as an usher, proudly introduced us to several associates. He said that we were the only ones to attend of those he had invited. I was pleased to have the opportunity to show that we had similar beliefs and appreciations.

***

Just when I was thinking that I was doing pretty well for an old guy, I find otherwise. Last night while watching tv, I kicked off my sandals and raised the footrest on the recliner. The sock on one of my feet was off. I lowered the footrest to get the missing sock but could not find it. After searching under the chair, around the chair and everywhere including the kitchen, the garage, bathroom and everywhere I had been, I gave up. After Mariann had conducted a futile search, she asked if I had looked under the bedclothes. Although I had a nap that day, I don't get under the covers during the day. That night I pulled down the covers and—there was the sock! I had been wearing just one sock all day even outside in the freezing cold with a barefoot in the open sandals. Apparently, my feet and my brain are both calcifying.

***

At 83 years of age Mariann is still an attractive woman. Recently, while we were in a restaurant booth, a woman approached and told me how lucky I was to have Mariann. I wondered what the woman was thinking. Was it my looks? Later at home, I looked in a mirror. I hadn't changed. Was I wrong all along thinking I was nice looking?

***

My early life seemed to indicate that I had a warrior personality. I believe that in later life Mariann developed a trooper personality. My mother often used the expression, "Like a trooper." I haven't heard that said for quite a while and the expression may now be archaic. Mom used the expression referring to those that kept doing their job despite difficulty. Mariann has withstood more than a fair share of setbacks and is still contending "like a trooper."

169

I thank God for Mariann, and I am grateful that Mariann has a strong, unwavering faith in God.

Fritz/Gerald Saga "Lessons Learned"

When I was six years old, I fell backwards while side stepping along a porch railing. My feet were under the bottom cross piece and only one foot pulled free as I fell backwards. While dangling upside down, I jerked my body until the foot came loose and I fell into the thick bushes below. Many years later I was reminded of that time as I cut a young deer free from a barbed wire fence. Its rear leg was caught just above the hoof as it tried to jump over the fence. I do not know how the top wire wraps around the leg, but it is not uncommon.

After cutting the deer free with the wire cutters I kept in the pickup, the deer hobbled away just as I had limped away from the porch many years before. It is not only the young that learn the hard way, it also happens with adults at any age. As an adult, I've had several mishaps with my eyes, and it is a wonder that I can still see well. Twice I had acid from a carboy in the shop squirt in my eye. It took the second such experience for me to learn to be more careful. The doctor that examined my eye after one of times said I had lost several tissues covering the eyeball. That must have been the second time it happened. Next, my left eyeball was pierced by a large thorn while I was pushing through thick brush when hunting woodcock. A doctor anesthetized the area and clamped the eye open before sewing the wound shut. I could see the needle sewing up the eyeball as he worked.

Years later, while pulling fence posts out of the ground by hand, I burst capillaries behind the right eyeball. A specialist said I probably would lose the sight in the eye, but I still see pretty well. Mariann said God threw away the mold after making me because I required too many Guardian Angels. Hopefully, some are still on the job.

Anecdote

Observing wildlife was convenient for us first while at Timber Trail then at Brookside followed by living at Apple Canyon Lake and finally alongside the arsenal grounds in Huntsville, Alabama. We learned that cottontail rabbits will eat bark later in the winter causing their flesh to be less suitable for the table. Rabbit hunters take notice and gardeners fence in your woody plants for the winter.

Hunters know that gray squirrels are more wary than are fox squirrels and grays are cleverer at frustrating efforts at keeping them off bird feeders. With some people it is a never-ending game trying new ways to thwart their depredations and gray squirrels may even chew a hole in a house to get in the attic during winter.

Crows, ravens and parrots are known to be clever. Starlings and mockingbirds are also clever and quite wary. Starlings, as nuisance birds are conditioned to being wary but to my knowledge, mockers have not been discriminated against.

At Timber Trail we watched Great Blue herons standing

motionless in shallow water waiting for a proper size fish or frog and a mother wood duck leading her brood to water after the ducklings had jumped from a hollow high in a tree. We had flying squirrels gliding through our woods and one evening we witnessed the territorial battle between two Great Horned owls. The next morning one of the owls was found dead.

In the spring and again in the fall we heard the whistling of Sandhill Cranes as these elegant birds flew in a long line high above us. At Brookside, several times we watched a migrating Osprey hovering high above our trout pond looking for the right size trout. The trout were too big, and the hawk left empty clawed. There, we chased away pesky Robins pecking away at their images in the glass doors and the crows bent on taking eggs or hatchlings from the nests of songbirds.

Some people had problems with woodpeckers drilling holes in the sides of their houses. One couple was so annoyed they erected netting around their house. Fortunately, woodpeckers spared us, and we fed them along with the other birds.

At our Brookside B&B, we had feeders on the deck outside the glass doors of the breakfast area. The lodge was situated at the edge of the woods with fields below, so we had numerous woodland birds as well as other birds at the feeders. All but the ground feeding catbirds, robins, thrushes and brown thrashers used the elevated feeders. The hummingbird feeder was in frequent use by Ruby Throated Hummers.

Because of the constant stream of ants using the hanging chord to get at the sugar water, it became necessary to run the cord through a spray can lid filled with water. The underside of the lid had a compartment in the center allowing for a surrounding water-filled moat that ants could not cross.

Once two hummers flew into the glass with such force that both fell unconscious on the deck. Eventually they both recovered. Another time we were amused by a baby swallow that was afraid to leave the nest after its siblings had flown. The parents, constantly squeaking as they flew around the nest, finally encouraged the youngster to fly. Even more amusing were the cardinals that were frantically feeding seeds to a young cowbird they thought was their offspring. The fledgling with its fuzzy feathers puffed out looked bigger than its foster parents. When a cowbird lays its egg in another absent bird's nest, it may remove the egg that is being replaced. Some birds recognize the cowbird egg as being foreign and push it out of the nest. These cardinals had been fooled and they hatched the egg as their own.

During our B&B hosting days we participated in the Natural Area Guardians Bluebird Recovery Program. Since then, the beautiful, family devoted Bluebirds have been our favorites and there have been many Bluebird hatches in the nest boxes I built. These boxes have a 1.5-inch-wide entrance hole in front and a door on the side. The female tolerates the occasional opening of the door while she is on the nest and may even remain there with the door open while a quick inspection is made.

Normally, five light blue eggs are laid before the female begins incubating them. The eggs hatch in 12 to 14 days after the last egg is laid. It takes another 17 to 21 days for the young birds to fledge (fly) and both parents feed the hatchlings and remove the droppings from the nest. The parents continue to feed the young at times after they fledge even when the young are scattered about in different trees. Bluebirds do not eat the seeds we put in the feeders, as they prefer insects. We lure the entire family to an elevated platform just outside our picture window with mealy worms. The inexpensive freeze-dried worms can be purchased at Lowes, Home Depot, and wild bird and pet stores. Often the entire Bluebird family will be on the platform together and sometimes we see the male feed the female there as well as the youngsters. I remove the Bluebird nest after it is vacated, as recommended. In a few weeks the same couple will build a new nest in the same or another box. Sometimes they have three broods in a season starting in early Spring.

As I write this, Mariann and I are being entertained by a pair of Bluebirds flying back and forth from the feeder to their nest with mouthful of mealy worms. Soon a family of seven will be on the feeder. Observing nature has always been rewarding for us and is even more so now that we have extra time and a great view of nature through our picture window. The "experts" urge us all to keep pets for our mental health. Mariann and I no longer have a dog, but we do have numerous pets just outside our window.

Reflection

When I was young, drug addiction was rare. Neither I nor my acquaintances used drugs, not even marijuana. Now, millions in this country use illegal drugs regularly. Some are seriously addicted with little hope of recovery. Illegal drugs are harmful both physically and psychologically; they are a threat to all of us. There are thousands of drug related deaths in the United States every year.

Law enforcement agencies spend billions annually in the losing battle against illegal drug distribution. These drugs are costly to users and everyone involved in their supply realizes huge profits on sales. That is the reason so many young people are gang members. The lack of opportunity for young men in poverty-stricken areas makes them susceptible to selling illegal drugs. The problem should be addressed both with a job training program and also by taking profit out of the illegal drug business. Job training has been attempted but the huge profit in illegal drug sales remains unaffected.

A government program for providing certain of these drugs

with flexible pricing, flexible potency and weekly allocations to drug users would eventually win the war against illegal drug sales. Government drug dispensaries could also be used as detox clinics where addicts are treated with safer and gradually less potent drugs until cured. That function of the dispensaries alone could justify supplying inexpensive or even free drugs to some. Mass production by selected drug manufacturers could even warrant reducing the cost of all drugs to pharmacies.

To use dispensaries for the purchase of a limited supply of drugs, an I.D. card would be issued, and purchase records maintained. Those wishing not to go to the dispensary themselves could have a substitute person use the card for them. These dispensaries could wean some drug users off drugs entirely and with the use of safer, less potent drugs, would eventually ruin the illegal drug business. Gang violence and drug related murders would be curtailed to a large degree. Dispensaries would be protected by the police and located near police stations. Adjustments in price, quantity and frequency of purchase together with eligibility could be made as the program develops. These drugs would become popular for being safe, pure, inexpensive and legal. Such a program could save billions in fighting the drug war and also save the lives of many including those of law enforcement personnel. No doubt there would be criticism at first but before long the program would prove its worth. So far, nothing else has been effective in alleviating this very serious problem.

Reflection

Policemen typically have what I call a guardian warrior personality. They have a desire to help and protect others and willingly confront danger if necessary. Obviously, it is not the remuneration that attracts individuals to police work, the pay is never proportionate to the danger.

A few policemen may at times be overly aggressive either because it is their nature or more likely because of the difficult people they must deal with. The unselfish and heroic acts performed by the police greatly outweigh the claims of police brutality. Some people may have a negative opinion of the police due to reports by the news media suggesting police brutality. Unfortunately, such reports are often misleading due to the use of sensationalism practiced by members of the news media.

More police officers are shot and killed today than ever before. Don't be misled, support our protectors.

Reflection

We learn from our mistakes, but it is better to learn from the mistakes of others. Reading the right material and consulting with the right people helps us avoid making mistakes. I have never built on a flood plain or purchased a house with termite damage, wood rot or mold, but I did buy a house having a potential problem with trees and the potential problem became reality. It cost several thousand dollars to remove large trees that were blown down by the wind and others cut down to remove the hazard. Fortunately, none fell on our buildings.

Some people that bought a house built prior to 1978 learned belatedly that the paint on the walls contained dangerous amounts of lead. Deteriorating lead-based paint produces lead dust. Sanding, cutting and demolition causes hazardous lead dust. A certified risk assessor can tell if there is a problem and if so, what to do about it.

Electric wiring in older buildings can be a fire hazard. It is wise to consult an expert before to making a commitment to buy.

These memoirs are now concluded in the year 2018. It appears that at least for Mariann and I, the trials, triumphs, and adventures have come to an end. We are content here in the foothills of the Appalachians. This pace is slow, the people friendly, and the cost of living quite reasonable. So again, "All's well that ends well!"

~Bob Fitzgerald

Introduction to Pamphlet

I've been asked what life has taught me. Life has taught me to be tolerant but wary and judge others by what they do rather than what they say. Too many people are "groupies" and their main concern is to be accepted. They mimic the talk and actions of others. Jumping on the bandwagon can be a mistake. All bandwagons are not headed in the right direction.

Sometimes it is difficult to decide what side to take and then it is best to be neutral. I agree with our founding fathers who were opposed to political parties. Today the parties responsible for running the government too often put their parties' interests ahead of the country's.

The following reflections I recently had printed for distribution. My purpose was to respond to some one-sided reporting by the news media and to offer my suggestions for a better way to do some things. I might change my mind about certain things, but I am sure of one thing: it is important to be open minded.

Suggestions For The Protection Of Students

1) Bolts on the inside of classroom doors
2) Outside doors locked when classes begin
3) Use volunteers proficient with weapons and licensed by the local sheriff to guard students
4) Any considered a threat to the lives of others should be listed on a federal data bank
5) Pending gun sales and transfers should be reviewed by the local sheriff

School shootings have become a common occurrence. Most of the shooters are adolescent boys whose parents or guardians have failed to monitor them properly. Any guns in the home should be secured. Parents who fail to act responsibly should be held accountable if their child harms others. Some people are afraid of guns and for others owning a gun for self-defense is necessary for peace of mind. A significant number of Americans own a gun. The great majority of these are good people and their gun ownership helps discourage some crimes.

Is our society becoming too permissive of the violence and obscene talk now prevalent in movies and TV? Psychologists agree that constant exposure to violence and vile language eventually makes it more acceptable to some people. Since the portrayal of violence and the use of obscene talk and action is legal our option is to discourage its proliferation any way we can.

When questioned or restrained by police, it is wise to do as directed. The officer has the legal right to require compliance with his orders; refusal can provoke anger and result in another "police brutality" news story. The news media feeds on suggestions of police brutality and by arousing public ire, more defiance to police is assured.

The majority of law enforcement officers do their job well. Of course, there are some complaints. Most often the complaints concern being disrespected or abused while being questioned. Now that the police have cameras to record the proceedings the facts will be known.

Is the motivation for the Black Lives Matter protest valid? Although violent crime by blacks is equal to that of whites, only 266 blacks were killed by police in 2016 compared to 573 whites killed. These statistics were compiled by the "Guardian" British news. The United States news media has not reported these figures by all accounts.

Some of us may object to people coming in large number to the United States today but the diversity and talent of our population is one reason for our leadership in the world. Acceptance of different cultures may take time but as a cohesive people we become more specialized and even more special.

Some people claim they do not believe in God or they don't believe in religion or both. Religious teachings stress forgiveness, tolerance, and care of others. All of us, including non-believers, benefit from these practices. Skeptics therefore must at least believe in the positive effect of religion.

Some people continue to advise us that you only get what you pay for; implying that we must pay more for good quality items. Most of us know this isn't always true. The well-meant advice is another reminder of Abraham Lincoln's admonishment, to not believe everything we hear.

Now that marijuana is being made legal in some states, there will be more injuries and deaths caused by impaired users. At what point will the volume of injuries and deaths exceed the value of the taxes realized from the marijuana sales?

The founding fathers of our country did not believe in the party system of government we have today. Some free thinkers now also prefer a no party system wherein legislators vote only according to their own opinions.

The Electoral College helps lessen the disadvantage small states have in electing a president due to the smaller total of their popular votes. The Electoral College is comprised of a number electors for each state proportionate to the number of their congressmen plus the two senators common to all states. This makes it possible for a few small states with a combined population less than a large state to outvote the large state.

Should Robert E. Lee's statue be banned from public property?

At the time of the Civil War people still had strong loyal ties to their home state. When invaded by northern troops they fought not for slavery but to defend their homeland. Only a small percentage of southerners owned slaves and Lee had long since freed the slaves he inherited.

Because of the overcrowding of prisons and the high cost of housing prisoners, some prison sentences have proven to be too short. Released prisoners often continue to commit crimes, including murder. The well-known, low maintenance tent prison in Arizona could be a solution to both overcrowding and the cost of housing.

The United States court system relies on jurors to decide the fate of the accused. This method has proven to be unreliable. Jurors, due to their own bias, lack of judgment, and sometimes dishonesty, have allowed the guilty to go free and the innocent condemned to prison. A system of three reputable judges to decide the fate of the accused would be better.

All religions that most of us are familiar with, emphasize the same principles, honor the Almighty by loving and caring for others. Since we all believe in these principles there should be no criticism of other religions. Instead, we should all be grateful that we share the same encouragement to love and care for each other.

Sometimes we are "turned off" by another's lack of intellect. People who are considered slow witted, lacking in knowledge, or just plain stupid, often have an exceptional talent or two. In some ways we are all both "dumb and smart."

Those who disapprove of hunting might consider that most wildlife die of starvation, disease or while being torn apart and possibly eaten alive by a predator. Would that realization diminish some of the negative opinion of hunters?

To love others and care for the needy is one of the major tenets of religions. Perhaps the best ways to judge the effectiveness of a religion is how well its followers practice these teachings. By this measurement, some atheists and agnostics would qualify as religious.

Some scientists claim disbelief in a creator yet believe in the symmetry of the universe. Is it then possible that all the harmony and beauty in nature plus the instinct and intellect of animals, including humans, is merely coincidence?

When considering whether to allow another to go ahead of us, we should also consider those behind us. Our good intention could cause resentment from others that are affected.

A common question concerning the relative intelligence of the sexes has an obvious answer: Some men are smarter than some women and some women are smarter than some men.

Those that protest honoring George Washington and Thomas Jefferson because they kept slaves should consider that at that time it may have been the more compassionate thing to do.

Rules of the Road

Keep to the right except when passing. All states mandate that the left lane of the road should be left open for passing. Violation of this regulation can result in an accident or "road rage" situation.

In heavy traffic, vehicles in the left hand should move faster than vehicles in the other lane.

***

The preceding reprint of my pamphlet includes a paragraph regarding the Black Lives Matter protest before NFL football games while the national anthem is sung. Considering that police patrols concentrate on ghettos where crime is rampant and that more than twice as many whites as blacks are killed by police, some fans wonder if the protests are justified. It would be interesting to learn what other blacks think about the protests; particularly some of the more experienced and knowledgeable former NFL football stars like Mike Strahan and Wade, commentator for HLN.

If the pamphlet is reprinted, the following will be included: Prisoners confined in desert-tent compounds could be put to work sorting plastic refuse salvaged from the oceans. Also, to help low income families, luxury items should be taxed more so that necessity items can be taxed less or not at all. Basic food and clothing should be in the low tax category and nonessential items in the higher tax group. Higher taxed items might include new cars, boats, guns, recreational items, liquor, tobacco, jewelry, gourmet food and restaurant purchases.

The pamphlet was sent to more than twenty radio and TV news stations and talk shows. The cover letter suggested passing along the thoughts on protecting school children from shooters. This was done shortly after the Parkland school shooting disaster. There has been no response from the stations and no mention on the air of the suggestions in the pamphlet.

Months later I volunteered to join a discussion organized by the Media Group of Alabama. It was represented to be a national survey to determine what Americans thought about gun control. I was partnered with a gentleman having views differing from my own. Our correspondence was channeled through the media group to us. After several weeks, all contact ceased without explanation. Several times I requested a report on the results of the survey; both by letter and by phone. Again, no response. Finally, I phoned the president of the media group and left a message. After more than a week without a response, I wrote to more than a dozen news stations asking about the survey. Again...no response! Obviously, some of these people are not as ethical as a lot of us might have assumed they were.

Wind Resistant Homes

Over the years I have been interested in concrete dome homes for the protection afforded from tornados, hurricanes, and fire. While visiting a number of dome homes and talking with the owners, I found that invariably they are pleased with the protection provided by their domes as well as the significantly reduced costs of heating, cooling, and maintenance.

Years ago, I spoke with David South, president of Monolithic construction. David has built concrete dome homes all over the United States and in several other countries. Several of David's clients lived through devastating tornados without significant damage to their concrete domes.

The cost of constructing a concrete dome house is comparable to the cost of a conventional stick-built house. In spite of the considerable protection provided by dome construction, it is seldom employed even in areas that have been devastated by wind or fire. What IS the reason for the avoidance? My guess is that most people don't know or don't think about this option in the time of need. Builders may be hesitant about trying new construction techniques and some people might think the appearance of the dome house is odd and not in harmony with other houses.

Recently Mariann and I went to see a modified version of a concrete dome house situated on Lookout Mountain near Chattanooga,

Tennessee. A good part of one side of the dome facing south is open. The prevailing wind is from the west and the interior of the house is sheltered from all but the rare south wind. This partial dome is attractive, but the construction process is lengthy and specialized as with all concrete dome houses. In one method, each coat of cement is sprayed on the rubberized inflated canvas form (with rebars affixed) and requires thirty days drying time between each successive coat. The same interval applies to the foam spraying of the interior. The time element and the specialized construction requirements for concrete dome houses can be a problem for timely rebuilding when homes are destroyed by wind or fire.

There are also stick-built house designs available for houses that are more wind resistant. Construction drawings for such homes can be obtained from a few architects or through the publisher of this book.

Undoubtedly in time dome buildings and other wind and fire-resistant buildings will more often be the building of choice. It seems that things often get better for those that are open to change.

For more information on wind resistant homes contact the publisher at **www.cbapub.com.**

Final Thoughts

Remember to take snapshots of special moments with dates and notes on the back. You will then be able to relive those times in later life.

I've been asked what life has taught me. It should teach tolerance if not love. It's difficult to love certain individuals.

I judge people more by what they do than by what they say. It's important to analyze a controversial subject before taking a side. Sometimes it may be difficult to decide, then it's best to "wait and see." Too many people are groupies and their main concern is to be "accepted." They mimic the talk and actions of others. Jumping on the "band wagon" can be a mistake. All band wagons are not headed in the right direction.

I agree with the founding fathers who were opposed to political parties. Today, the parties responsible for running the government too often put their party's interests ahead of the country's.

I consider myself an independent voter but I usually vote for the conservative candidate. Recently I was swayed by the rhetoric of a professed liberal and rhetoric was all it turned out to be. There were no substantive results.

Believing persuasive people can be a mistake Abraham Lincoln said, "Believe half of what you see and none of what you hear." Of course, he simply meant for us to avoid being gullible. Thoughtful judgment helps us and makes our country better.

All's Well That Ends Well!

Waterfall built by Bob in 2017

By authority of the Board of Trustees of the

UNIVERSITY OF ILLINOIS

and upon recommendation of the University Senate

Robert Edward Fitzgerald

has been admitted to the Degree of

Bachelor of Science

from the Division of Special Services for War Veterans

and is entitled to all rights and honors thereto appertaining

Witness the Seal of the University and the signatures of its Officers
this _twelfth_ day of February, nineteen hundred and fifty-four.

President of the Board of Trustees

Secretary of the Board of Trustees

President of the University

Military Service

William Fitzgerald II	Navy 1944
Robert Fitzgerald	Army 1950
Richard Fitzgerald	Navy 1956
Michael Fitzgerald	Navy 1982
William Fitzgerald III	Marines 1982

Athletic Achievement

William Fitzgerald II

1943 High School Football National Champs

Richard Fitzgerald

1951 Illinois Football High Scorer

Notre Dame

Chicago Bears

Robert Fitzgerald

1943 1st Place Chicago City Long Jump

William Fitzgerald III

Minnesota State 60 Yard Dash Record

Steven Fitzgerald 1978-81

Colorado All State Hockey and Football

Ryan Fitzgerald 2013-15

Colorado All State Football and La Crosse

Lisa Duerr

College Volleyball Scholarship

Christine Duerr

College Volleyball Scholarship

Jennifer Duerr

College Volleyball Scholarship

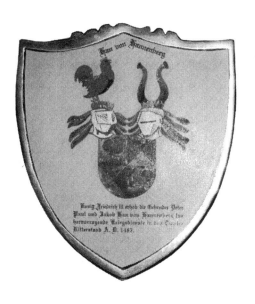

Made in the USA
Columbia, SC
31 December 2019